the life-changing magic of tidying up

TRANSLATED
FROM THE
JAPANESE BY
CATHY HIRANO

the life-changing magic of tidying up

the Japanese art of decluttering
and organizing

marie kondo

TEN SPEED PRESS
BERKELEY

Contents

2

Finish discarding first 33

3

Tidying by category works like magic 63

4

Storing your things to make your life shine 129

5
—

The magic of tidying dramatically transforms your life 173

Introduction

In this book, I have summed up how to put your space in order in a way that will change your life forever.

Impossible? A common response and not surprising, considering that almost everyone has experienced a rebound effect at least once, if not multiple times, after tidying.

Have *you* ever tidied madly, only to find that all too soon your home or workspace is cluttered again? If so, let me share with you the secret of success. **Start by discarding. Then organize your space, thoroughly, completely, in one go.** If you adopt this approach—the KonMari Method—you'll never revert to clutter again.

Although this approach contradicts conventional wisdom, everyone who completes my private course has successfully kept their house in order—with unexpected results. Putting their house in order positively affects all other aspects of their lives, including work and family. Having devoted more than 80 percent of my life to this subject, I *know* that tidying can transform your life.

Does it still sound too good to be true? If your idea of tidying is getting rid of one unnecessary item a day or cleaning up your room a little at a time, then you are right. It won't have much effect on your life. If you change your approach, however, tidying can have an immeasurable impact. In fact, that is what it means to put your house in order.

I started reading home and lifestyle magazines when I was five, and it was this that inspired me, from the age of fifteen, to undertake a serious study of tidying that led to my development of the KonMari Method (based on a combination of my first and last names). I am now a consultant and spend most of my days visiting homes and offices, giving hands-on advice to people who find it difficult to tidy, who tidy but suffer rebounds, or who want to tidy but don't know where to start.

The number of things my clients have discarded, from clothes and undergarments to photos, pens, magazine clippings, and makeup samples, easily exceeds a million items. This is no exaggeration. I have assisted individual clients who have thrown out two hundred 45-liter garbage bags in one go.

From my exploration of the art of organizing and my experience helping messy people become tidy, there is one thing I can say with confidence: **A dramatic reorganization**

of the home causes correspondingly dramatic changes in lifestyle and perspective. It is life transforming. I mean it. Here are just a few of the testimonies I receive on a daily basis from former clients.

> *After your course, I quit my job and launched my own business doing something I had dreamed of doing ever since I was a child.*
>
> ———
>
> *Your course taught me to see what I really need and what I don't. So I got a divorce. Now I feel much happier.*
>
> ———
>
> *Someone I have been wanting to get in touch with recently contacted me.*
>
> ———
>
> *I'm delighted to report that since cleaning up my apartment, I've been able to really increase my sales.*
>
> ———
>
> *My husband and I are getting along much better.*
>
> ———
>
> *I'm amazed to find that just throwing things away has changed me so much.*
>
> ———
>
> *I finally succeeded in losing ten pounds.*

My clients always sound so happy, and the results show that tidying has changed their way of thinking and their approach to life. In fact, it has changed their future.

Why? This question is addressed in more detail through-out the book, but basically, **when you put your house in order, you put your affairs and your past in order, too.** As a result, you can see quite clearly what you need in life and what you don't, and what you should and shouldn't do.

I currently offer a course for clients in their homes and for company owners in their offices. These are all private, one-on-one consultations, but I have yet to run out of clients. There is currently a three-month waiting list, and I receive inquiries daily from people who have been introduced by a former client or who have heard about the course from someone else. I travel from one end of Japan to the other and sometimes even overseas. Tickets for one of my public talks for stay-at-home parents sold out overnight. There was a waiting list not only for cancellations but also for the waiting list. Yet my repeater rate is zero. From a business perspective, this would appear to be a fatal flaw. But what if my lack of repeaters was actually the secret to the popularity of my approach?

As I said at the beginning, people who use the KonMari Method never revert to clutter again. Because they can keep their space in order, they don't need to come back for more lessons. I occasionally check in with graduates of my courses to see how they are doing. In almost every case, not only is their home or office still in order but they are continuing to improve their space. It is evident from the photographs they send that they have even fewer belongings than when they finished the course, and have acquired new curtains and furnishings. **They are surrounded only by the things they love.**

Why does my course transform people? Because my approach is not simply a technique. The act of tidying is a series of simple actions in which objects are moved from one place to another. It involves putting things away where they belong. This seems so simple that even a six-year-old should be able to do it. Yet most people can't. A short time after tidying, their space is a disorganized mess. The cause is not lack of skills but rather lack of awareness and the inability to make tidying a regular habit. In other words, the root of the problem lies in the mind. Success is 90 percent dependent on our mind-set. Excluding the fortunate few to whom organizing comes naturally, if we do not address this aspect, rebound is inevitable no matter how much is discarded or how cleverly things are organized.

So how can you acquire the right kind of mind-set? There is just one way, and, paradoxically, it is by acquiring the right technique. Remember: the KonMari Method I describe in this book is not a mere set of rules on how to sort, organize, and put things away. It is a guide to acquiring the right mind-set for creating order and becoming a tidy person.

Of course, I can't claim that all my students have perfected the art of tidying. Unfortunately, some had to stop for one reason or another before completing the course. And some quit because they expected me to do the work for them. As an organizing fanatic and professional, I can tell you right now that no matter how hard I try to organize another's space, no matter how perfect a storage system I devise, I can never put someone else's house in order in the true sense of the term. Why? Because a person's awareness and perspective on his or her own lifestyle are far more important than any skill at sorting, storing, or whatever. Order is dependent on the extremely personal values of what a person wants to live with.

Most people would prefer to live in a clean and tidy space. Anyone who has managed to tidy even once will have wished to keep it that way. But many don't believe it's possible. They try out various approaches to tidying only to find that things soon return to "normal." I am absolutely convinced, however, that everyone can keep his or her space in order.

To do that, it is essential to thoroughly reassess your habits and assumptions about tidying. That may sound like far too much work, but don't worry. By the time you finish reading this book, you will be ready and willing. People often tell me, "I'm disorganized by nature," "I can't do it," or "I don't have time"; but being messy is not hereditary nor is it related to lack of time. It has far more to do with the accumulation of mistaken notions about tidying, such as "it's best to tackle one room at a time" or "it's better to do a little each day" or "storage should follow the flow plan of the house."

In Japan, people believe that things like cleaning your room and keeping your bathroom spick-and-span bring good luck, but if your house is cluttered, the effect of polishing the toilet bowl is going to be limited. The same is true for the practice of feng shui. It is only when you put your house in order that your furniture and decorations come to life.

When you've finished putting your house in order, your life will change dramatically. Once you have experienced what it's like to have a truly ordered house, you'll feel your whole world brighten. Never again will you revert to clutter. This is what I call **the magic of tidying.** And the effects are stupendous. Not only will you never be messy again, but you'll also get a new start on life. This is the magic I want to share with as many people as possible.

1

Why can't I keep my house in order?

You can't tidy if you've never learned how

When I tell people that my profession is teaching others how to tidy, I am usually met with looks of astonishment. "Can you actually make money doing that?" is their first question. This is almost always followed by, "Do people need lessons in tidying?"

It's true that while instructors and schools offer courses in everything from cooking and how to wear a kimono to yoga and Zen meditation, you'll be hard-pressed to find classes on how to tidy. The general assumption, in Japan at least, is that tidying doesn't need to be taught but rather is picked up naturally. Cooking skills and recipes are passed down as family traditions from grandmother to mother to daughter, yet one never hears of anyone passing on the family secrets of tidying, even within the same household.

Think back to your own childhood. I'm sure most of us have been scolded for not tidying up our rooms, but how many of our parents consciously taught us how to tidy as part of our upbringing? Our parents demanded that we clean up our rooms, but they, too, had never been trained in how to do that. When it comes to tidying, we are all self-taught.

Instruction in tidying is neglected not only in the home but also at school. When we think back to our home economics classes, most of us remember making hamburgers or learning how to use a sewing machine to make an apron, but compared to cooking and sewing, surprisingly little time is devoted to the subject of tidying. Even if it is included in a textbook, that section is either just read in class, or worse, assigned for reading at home so that students can skip ahead to more popular topics, such as food and health. Consequently, even the extremely rare home economics graduates who have formally studied "tidying" can't do it.

Food, clothing, and shelter are the most basic human needs, so you would think that where we live would be considered just as important as what we eat and what we wear. Yet in most societies tidying, the job that keeps a home livable, is completely disregarded because of the misconception that the ability to tidy is acquired through experience and therefore doesn't require training.

Do people who have been tidying for more years than others tidy better? The answer is no. Twenty-five percent of my students are women in their fifties, and the majority of them have been homemakers for close to thirty years, which makes them veterans at this job. But do they tidy better than women in their twenties? The opposite is true. Many of them have spent so many years applying erroneous conventional approaches that their homes overflow with unnecessary items and they struggle to keep clutter under control with ineffective storage methods. How can they be expected to know how to tidy when they have never studied it properly?

If you, too, don't know how to tidy, don't be discouraged. Now is the time to learn. By studying and applying the KonMari Method presented in this book, you can escape the vicious cycle of clutter.

A tidying marathon doesn't cause rebound

"I clean up when I realize how untidy my place is, but once I'm done, it's not long before it's a mess again." This is a common complaint, and the standard response touted by magazine advice columns is, "Don't try tidying your entire house all at once. You'll just rebound. Make a habit of doing a little at a time." I first stumbled across this refrain when I was five. As the middle child of three children, I was raised with a great deal of freedom. My mother was busy taking care of my newborn younger sister, and my brother, who was two years older than me, was always glued to the TV playing video games. Consequently, I spent most of my time at home on my own.

My favorite pastime was reading home and lifestyle magazines. My mother subscribed to *ESSE*—a magazine with features on interior decorating, cleaning tips, and product reviews. As soon as it was delivered, I would snatch it from the mailbox before my mother even knew it had arrived, rip open the envelope, and immerse myself in the contents. On my way home from school, I liked to stop at the bookstore and browse through *Orange Page*, a popular Japanese food magazine. I wasn't actually able to read all the words, but these magazines, with their photos of scrumptious dishes, amazing tips for removing stains and grease, and penny-saving ideas, were as fascinating for me as game guides were for my brother. I would fold the corner of a page that caught my interest and dream of trying out the tip described.

I also made up a variety of my own solitary "games." For example, after reading a feature on saving money, I immediately launched into a "power-saving game" that involved roaming about the house and unplugging things that weren't in use, even though I knew nothing about electric meters. In response to another feature, I filled plastic bottles with water and put them in the toilet tank in a solo "water-saving contest." Articles on storage inspired me to convert milk cartons into dividers for my drawers and make a letter rack by stacking empty video cases between two pieces of furniture. At school, while other kids were playing dodgeball or skipping, I'd slip away to rearrange the bookshelves in our classroom, or check the contents of the mop cupboard, all the while muttering about the poor storage methods. "If only there were an S-hook, it would be so much easier to use."

But there was one problem that seemed unsolvable. No matter how much I tidied, it wasn't long before every space was a mess again. The milk carton dividers in my desk drawer soon overflowed with pens. The rack made from video cases was soon so crammed with letters and papers that it crumpled to the floor. With cooking or sewing, practice makes perfect, but even though tidying is also housework, I never seemed to improve no matter how often I did it—nowhere stayed tidy for long.

"It can't be helped," I consoled myself. "Rebound comes with the territory. If I tackle the job all at once, I'll just get discouraged." I had read this in many articles about tidying and assumed it was true. If I had a time machine now, I'd go back and tell myself, "That's wrong. If you use the right approach, you'll never rebound."

Most people associate the word "rebound" with dieting, but when they hear it used in the context of tidying, it still makes sense. It seems logical that a sudden, drastic reduction in clutter could have the same effect as a drastic cut in calories. But don't be deceived. The moment you begin moving furniture around and getting rid of garbage, your room changes. It's very simple. If you put your house in order in one fell swoop, you will have tidied up in one fell swoop. (In Japanese, the term is *ikki ni*, or "in one go.") Rebound occurs because people mistakenly believe they have tidied thoroughly, when in fact they have only sorted and stored things halfway. If you put your house in order properly, you'll be able to keep your room tidy, even if you are lazy or sloppy by nature.

Tidy a little a day and you'll be tidying forever

"If you tidy your house all at once, you'll rebound. It's better to make it a habit to do a little at a time." Although this advice sounds very tempting, we've already seen that the first part is wrong. How about the suggestion that we should do only a little a day? Although it sounds convincing, don't be fooled. The reason you never seem to finish is precisely because you tidy a little at a time.

Changing lifestyle habits acquired over a span of many years is generally extremely difficult. If you have never succeeded in staying tidy to date, you will find it next to impossible to develop the habit of tidying a little at a time. **People cannot change their habits without first changing their way of thinking.** And that's not easy! After all, it's quite hard to control what we think. There is, however, one way to drastically transform the way we think about tidying.

The subject of tidying first caught my attention when I was in junior high school. The catalyst was a book called *The Art of Discarding* by Nagisa Tatsumi (Takarajimasha, Inc.), which explained the importance of getting rid of unnecessary things. I picked the book up on my way home from school, intrigued to see a topic I had never encountered before, and I can still remember the shock of surprise I felt as I read it on the train. I became so absorbed that I almost missed my stop. Once home, I went straight to my room with a handful of garbage bags and stayed closeted for several hours. Although my room was small, by the time I finished I had eight bags full of stuff—clothes I never wore, textbooks from elementary school, toys I had not played with in years, my eraser and seal collection. I had forgotten that most of these things even existed. I sat motionless on the floor for about an hour afterward staring at the pile of bags and wondering, "Why on earth did I bother keeping all this stuff?"

What shocked me most, however, was how different my room looked. After only a few hours, I could see parts of the floor that had never been revealed before. My room seemed to have been transformed, and the air inside seemed so much fresher and brighter that even my mind felt clearer. Tidying, I realized, could have far more impact than I had ever imagined. Thunderstruck by the extent of the change, from that day on I turned my attention from cooking and sewing, which I had thought were the essentials of a well-kept home, to the art of tidying.

Tidying brings visible results. Tidying never lies. The ultimate secret of success is this: **If you tidy up in one shot, rather than little by little, you can dramatically change your mind-set.** A change so profound that it touches your emotions will irresistibly affect your way of thinking and your lifestyle habits. My clients do not develop the habit of tidying gradually. Every one of them has been clutter-free since they undertook their tidying marathon. This approach is the key to preventing rebound.

When people revert to clutter no matter how much they tidy, it is not their room or their belongings but their way of thinking that is at fault. Even if they are initially inspired, they can't stay motivated and their efforts peter out. The root cause lies in the fact that they can't see the results or feel the effects. This is precisely why success depends on experiencing tangible results immediately. **If you use the right method and concentrate your efforts on eliminating clutter thoroughly and completely within a short span of time, you'll see instant results that will empower you to keep your space in order ever after.** Anyone who experiences this process, no matter who they are, will vow never to revert to clutter again.

Why you should aim for perfection

"Don't aim for perfection. Start off slowly and discard just one item a day." What lovely words to ease the hearts of those who lack confidence in their ability to tidy. I came across this advice when I was devouring every book about tidying that had ever been published in Japan, and I fell for it, hook, line, and sinker. The momentum sparked by my epiphany concerning the power of tidying was beginning to wear off, and I was starting to feel jaded by the lack of solid results. These words seemed to make sense. It seems daunting to aim for perfection from the beginning. Besides, perfection is supposedly unattainable. By discarding one thing a day, I could get rid of 365 things by the end of the year.

Convinced that I had discovered a very practical method, I immediately followed the book's instructions. I opened my closet in the morning wondering what to dispose of that day. Seeing a T-shirt that I no longer wore, I put it in the garbage bag. Before going to bed the next night, I opened my desk drawer and discovered a notebook that seemed too childish for me. I put it in the bag. Noticing a memo pad in the same drawer, I thought to myself, "Oh, I don't need that anymore," but as I reached out to pick it up, I paused at a new thought. "I can save that to discard tomorrow." And I waited until the next morning to throw it away. The day after that, I forgot completely, so I got rid of two items on the following day.

To be honest, I did not last two weeks. I am not the type of person who likes to plug away at something, one step at a time. For people like me, who do their assignments on the very last day right before the deadline, this approach just doesn't work. Besides, casting off one object a day did not compensate for the fact that when I shop, I buy several items at one time. In the end, the pace at which I reduced could not keep up with the pace at which I acquired new things, and I was confronted with the discouraging fact that my space was still cluttered. It wasn't long before I had completely forgotten to follow the rule of discarding one item per day.

So I can tell you from experience that you will never get your house in order if you only clean up half-heartedly. If, like me, you are not the diligent, persevering type, then I recommend aiming for perfection just once. Many people may protest when I use the word "perfection," insisting that it's an impossible goal. But don't worry. Tidying in the end is just a physical act. The work involved can be broadly divided into two kinds: deciding whether or not to dispose of something and deciding where to put it. If you can do these two things, you can achieve perfection. Objects can be counted. All you need to do is look at each item, one at a time, and decide whether or not to keep it and where to put it. That's all you need to do to complete this job. It is not hard to tidy up perfectly and completely in one fell swoop. In fact, anyone can do it. And if you want to avoid rebound, this is the only way to do it.

The moment you start you reset your life

Have you ever found yourself unable to study the night before an exam and begun frantically tidying? I confess, I have. In fact, for me it was a regular event. I would take the piles of handouts covering my desk and throw them in the garbage. Then, unable to stop, I'd tackle the textbooks and papers littering the floor and begin arranging them in my bookcase. Finally, I'd open my desk drawer and start organizing my pens and pencils. Before I knew it, it would be two-thirty in the morning. Overcome by sleep, I'd jolt awake again at five and only then, in a complete panic, would I open my textbook and buckle down to study.

I thought that this urge to tidy before an exam was a peculiar quirk of my own, but after meeting many others who do the same, I realized that it was a common phenomenon. Many people get the urge to clean up when under pressure, such as just before an exam. But this urge doesn't occur because they want to clean their room. It occurs because they need to put "something else" in order. Their brain is actually clamoring to study, but when it notices the cluttered space, the focus switches to "I need to clean up my room." The fact that the tidying urge rarely continues once the crisis is over proves my theory. Once the exam has ended, the passion poured into cleaning the previous night dissipates and life returns to normal. All thought of tidying is wiped from the person's mind. Why? Because the problem faced—that is, the need to study for the exam—has been "tidied away."

This doesn't mean that tidying your room will actually calm your troubled mind. While it may help you feel refreshed temporarily, the relief won't last because you haven't addressed the true cause of your anxiety. If you let the temporary relief achieved by tidying up your physical space deceive you, you will never recognize the need to clean up your psychological space. This was true for me. Distracted by the "need" to tidy my room, it took me so long to get down to studying that my grades were always terrible.

Let's imagine a cluttered room. It does not get messy all by itself. You, the person who lives in it, makes the mess. There is a saying that "a messy room equals a messy mind." I look at it this way. When a room becomes cluttered, the cause is more than just physical. Visible mess helps distract us from the true source of the disorder. The act of cluttering is really an instinctive reflex that draws our attention away from the heart of an issue.

If you can't feel relaxed in a clean and tidy room, try confronting your feeling of anxiety. It may shed light on what is really bothering you. When your room is clean and uncluttered, you have no choice but to examine your inner state. You can see any issues you have been avoiding and are forced to deal with them. From the moment you start tidying, you will be compelled to reset your life. As a result, your life will start to change. That's why the task of putting your house in order should be done quickly. It allows you to confront the issues that are really important. **Tidying is just a tool, not the final destination.** The true goal should be to establish the lifestyle you want most once your house has been put in order.

Storage experts are hoarders

What is the first problem that comes to mind when you think of tidying? For many, the answer is storage. My clients often want me to teach them what to put where. Believe me, I can relate, but unfortunately, this is not the real issue. **A booby trap lies within the term "storage."** Features on how to organize and store your belongings and convenient storage products are always accompanied by stock phrases that make it sound simple, such as "organize your space in no time" or "make tidying fast and easy." It's human nature to take the easy route, and most people leap at storage methods that promise quick and convenient ways to remove visible clutter. I confess that I, too, was once captivated by the storage myth.

An avid fan of home and lifestyle magazines since kindergarten, I would read a feature on how to put things away and have to try out each suggestion immediately. I made drawers out of tissue boxes and broke my piggybank to purchase nifty storage items. In junior high on my way home from school, I would drop in at a DIY store or browse at a magazine stand to check out the latest products. In high school, I even called up the manufacturer of particularly intriguing items and pestered the receptionist to tell me the story of how they were invented. I dutifully used these storage items to organize my things. Then I would stand and admire my handiwork, content with how convenient the world had become. From this experience, I can honestly declare that storage methods do not solve the problem of how to get rid of clutter. In the end, they are only a superficial answer.

When I finally came to my senses, I saw that my room still wasn't tidy even though it was full of magazine racks, bookshelves, drawer dividers, and other storage units of every kind. "Why does my room still feel cluttered when I've worked so hard to organize and store things away?" I wondered. Filled with despair, I looked at the contents of each storage unit and had a flash of revelation. I didn't need most of the things that were in them! Although I thought that I had been tidying, in fact I had merely been wasting my time shoving stuff out of sight, concealing the things I didn't need under a lid. **Putting things away creates the illusion that the clutter problem has been solved.** But sooner or later, all the storage units are full, the room once again overflows with things, and some new and "easy" storage method becomes necessary, creating a negative spiral. This is why tidying must start with discarding. We need to exercise self-control and resist storing our belongings until we have finished identifying what we really want and need to keep.

Sort by category, not by location

My study of tidying began in earnest when I was in junior high and basically consisted of repeated practice. Every day I cleaned one place at a time—my own room, my brother's room, my sister's room, the bathroom. Each day I planned where to tidy and launched solo campaigns that resembled bargain sales. "The fifth of every month is 'living room day'!" "Today is 'clean the pantry day.'" "Tomorrow I conquer the bathroom cupboards!"

I maintained this custom even after entering high school. When I came home, I headed straight for the place I had decided to clean that day without even changing out of my school uniform. If my target was a set of plastic drawers in the washroom cupboard, I would open the doors and dump everything out of one of the drawers, including makeup samples, soaps, toothbrushes, and razors. Then I would sort them by category, organize them into box dividers, and return them to the drawer. Finally, I would gaze in quiet admiration at the neatly organized contents before going on to the next drawer. I would sit on the floor for hours sorting things in the cupboard until my mother called me for supper.

One day, I was sorting the contents of a drawer in the hall cupboard when I stopped in surprise. "This must be the same drawer that I cleaned yesterday," I thought. It wasn't, but the items inside were the same—makeup samples, soaps, toothbrushes, and razors. I was sorting them by category, putting them in boxes, and returning them to the drawer just like I had the day before. It was at this moment that it hit me: **Tidying up by location is a fatal mistake.** I'm ashamed to admit that it took me three years to see this.

Many people are surprised to hear that such a seemingly viable approach is actually a common pitfall. The root of the problem lies in the fact that people often store the same type of item in more than one place. When we tidy each place separately, we fail to see that we're repeating the same work in many locations and become locked into a vicious circle of tidying. To avoid this, I recommend tidying by category. For example, instead of deciding that today you'll tidy a particular room, set goals like "clothes today, books tomorrow." One reason so many of us never succeed at tidying is because we have too much stuff. This excess is caused by our ignorance of how much we actually own. When we disperse storage of a particular item throughout the house and tidy one place at a time, we can never grasp the overall volume and therefore can never finish. To escape this negative spiral, tidy by category, not by place.

Don't change the method to suit your personality

Handbooks for tidying often claim that the cause of clutter differs depending on the person, and that therefore we should select the method that best suits our personality type. At first glance, this argument seems convincing. "So that's why I can't seem to keep my space tidy," we might think. "The method I've been using doesn't suit my character." We can check the handy chart on what method works for lazy people, busy people, picky people, or nonpicky people, and choose the one that fits.

At one point, I explored this idea of categorizing methods of tidying by character type. I read books on psychology, interviewed my clients about their blood types, their parents' characters, and so on, and even tried a popular type of astrology called *Dobutsu uranai*, or zoological fortune-telling. I spent over five years analyzing my findings in my search for a general principle governing the best method for each personality type. Instead, I discovered that there is no point whatsoever in changing your approach to suit your personality. When it comes to tidying, the majority of people are lazy. They are also busy. As for being picky, everyone is particular about certain things but not about others. When I examined the personality categories suggested, I realized that I fit all of them. So by what standard was I to categorize people's reasons for being untidy?

I have a habit of trying to categorize everything, probably because I have spent so much time pondering how to organize. When I first started out as a consultant, I worked very hard to categorize my clients and tailor the content of my services to suit each type. In retrospect, however, I can see that I had an ulterior motive. Somehow I imagined that a complex approach consisting of different methods for different character types would make me look more professional. After careful consideration, however, I came to the conclusion that it makes far more sense to categorize people by their actions rather than by some generalized personality trait.

Using this approach, people who can't stay tidy can be categorized into just three types: the "can't-throw-it-away" type, the "can't-put-it-back" type, and the "first-two-combined" type. Looking at my clients, I further realized that 90 percent fall into the third category—the "can't-throw-it-away, can't-put-it-back" type—while the remaining 10 percent fall into the "can't-put-it-back" type. I have yet to find someone who is purely the "can't throw it away" type, probably because anyone who can't throw things away will soon end up with so much stuff that their storage space overflows. As for the 10 percent who can discard but can't put things away, when we start tidying seriously, it is soon obvious that they could discard much more because they produce at least thirty bags of garbage.

My point is that tidying must begin with discarding regardless of personality type. As long as my clients grasp this principle, there is no need for me to change the content of what I teach to suit the person. I teach the same approach to everyone. How I convey it and the way each client puts it into practice will naturally differ because each individual is just as unique as the way he or she furnishes the house. But I don't need to worry about identifying these differences or creating complex categories. **Effective tidying involves only two essential actions: discarding and deciding where to store things. Of the two, discarding must come first.** This principle does not change. The rest depends on the level of tidiness you personally want to achieve.

Make tidying a special event, not a daily chore

I begin my course with these words: **Tidying is a special event. Don't do it every day.** This usually elicits a moment of stunned silence. Of course, there are countless perspectives on tidying, and even though I have undertaken an exhaustive study of the subject, I don't claim to know every method that exists. Therefore, what I say here applies only to my own method. Still, let me repeat: tidying should be done just once. Or, to put it more accurately, the work of tidying should be completed once and for all within a single period of time.

If you think tidying is an endless chore that must be done every day, you are gravely mistaken. There are two types of tidying—"daily tidying" and "special event tidying." Daily tidying, which consists of using something and putting it back in its place, will always be part of our lives as long as we need to use clothes, books, writing materials, and so on. But the purpose of this book is to inspire you to tackle the "special event" of putting your house in order as soon as possible.

By successfully concluding this once-in-a-lifetime task, you will gain the lifestyle you aspire to and enjoy a clean and orderly space of your choosing. Can you place your hand on your heart and swear that you are happy when surrounded by so much stuff that you don't even remember what's there? Most people desperately need to put their house in order. Unfortunately, the majority of them fail to embrace this as a "special event" and instead make do with rooms that are more like storage sheds. Decades drag by as they struggle unsuccessfully to maintain order by tidying every day.

Believe me. Until you have completed the once-in-a-lifetime event of putting your house in order, any attempt to tidy on a daily basis is doomed to failure. Conversely, once you have put your house in order, tidying will be reduced to the very simple task of putting things back where they belong. In fact, this becomes an unconscious habit. I use the term "special event" because it is crucial to tackle this job within a short space of time while your spirits are uplifted. After all, it isn't desirable to stay in a state of excitement forever.

You may worry that even when this event is over your space will sink back into disorder. Perhaps you shop a lot and imagine that your possessions will just pile up again. I realize that it's hard to believe if you have never tried it, but once you have completed this dramatic cleanup, you will have no difficulty whatsoever in putting things back where they belong or in deciding where to keep new things. Unbelievable as it may sound, you only have to experience a state of perfect order once to be able to maintain it. All you need to do is take the time to sit down and examine each item you own, decide whether you want to keep or discard it, and then choose where to put what you keep.

Have you ever told yourself, "I'm just no good at tidying," or "It's not worth trying; I was born untidy"? Many people carry this type of negative self-image for years, but it is swept away the instant they experience their own perfectly clean space. This drastic change in self-perception, the belief that you can do anything if you set your mind to it, transforms behavior and lifestyles. This is precisely why my students never experience rebound. Once you have experienced the powerful impact of a perfectly ordered space, you, too, will never return to clutter. Yes, I mean you!

It may sound too difficult, but I can honestly say that it's quite simple. When you tidy, you are dealing with objects. Objects are easy to discard and move around.

Anyone can do it. **Your goal is clearly in sight. The moment you have put everything in its place, you have crossed the finish line.** Unlike work, studies, or sports, there is no need to compare your performance to that of anyone else. You are the standard. Better yet, the one thing that everyone finds hardest to do—continuing— is totally unnecessary. You only have to decide where to put things once.

I never tidy my room. Why? Because it is already tidy. The only tidying I do is once or sometimes twice a year, and for a total of about one hour each time. The many days I spent tidying without seeing permanent results now seem hard to believe. In contrast, I feel happy and content. I have time to experience bliss in my quiet space, where even the air feels fresh and clean; time to sit and sip herbal tea while I reflect on my day. As I look around, my glance falls on a painting that I particularly love, purchased overseas, and a vase of fresh flowers in one corner. Although not large, the space I live in is graced only with those things that speak to my heart. My life-style brings me joy.

Wouldn't you like to live this way, too? It's easy, once you know how to truly put your home in order.

2
—
Finish discarding first

Start by discarding, all at once, intensely and completely

You think you have tidied everything perfectly, but within a few days you notice that your room is becoming cluttered again. As time goes by, you collect more things, and before you know it, your space has reverted to its previous state. This rebound effect is caused by ineffective methods that tackle tidying only halfway. As I've already mentioned, there is just one way to escape this negative spiral—by tidying efficiently all at once, as quickly as possible, to make the perfect clutter-free environment. But how does this create the right mind-set?

When you tidy your space completely, you transform the scenery. The change is so profound that you feel as if you are living in a totally different world. This deeply affects your mind and inspires a strong aversion to reverting to your previously cluttered state. The key is to make the change so sudden that you experience a complete change of heart. The same impact can never be achieved if the process is gradual.

To achieve a sudden change like this, you need to use the most efficient method of tidying. Otherwise, before you know it, the day will be gone and you will have made no headway. The more time it takes, the more tired you feel, and the more likely you are to give up when you're only halfway through. When things pile up again, you will be caught in a downward spiral. From my experience with private individual lessons, "quickly" means about half a year. That may seem like a long time, but it is only six months out of your entire life. Once the process is complete and you've experienced what it's like to be perfectly tidy, you will have been freed forever from the mistaken assumption that you're no good at tidying.

For the best results, I ask that you adhere faithfully to the following rule: **Tidy in the right order.** As we've seen, there are only two tasks involved—discarding and deciding where to keep things. Just two, but discarding must come first. Be sure to completely finish the first task before starting the next. **Do not even think of putting your things away until you have finished the process of discarding.** Failure to follow this order is one reason many people never make permanent progress. In the middle of discarding, they start thinking about where to put things. As soon as they think, "I wonder if it will fit in this drawer," the work of discarding comes to a halt. You can think about where to put things when you've finished getting rid of everything you don't need.

To summarize, the secret of success is to tidy in one shot, as quickly and completely as possible, and to start by discarding.

Before you start, visualize your destination

By now you understand why it is crucial to discard before thinking about where to keep things. But to start discarding without thinking ahead at all would be like casting yourself into the negative spiral of clutter. Instead, begin by identifying your goal. There must have been some reason you picked up this book. What was it that motivated you to tidy in the first place? What do you hope to gain through tidying? Before you start getting rid of things, take the time to think this through carefully. This means visualizing the ideal lifestyle you dream of. If you skip this step, not only will it delay the whole process, but it will also put you at higher risk for rebound. Goals like "I want to live clutter-free" or "I want to be able to put things away" are too broad. You need to think much more deeply than that. **Think in concrete terms so that you can vividly picture what it would be like to live in a clutter-free space.**

One client in her twenties defined her dream as "a more feminine lifestyle." She lived in a messy seven-mat room (seven tatami mats take up about ten by thirteen feet of floor space) with a built-in closet and three sets of shelves of different sizes. This should have been sufficient storage space, but no matter which way I turned, all I could see was clutter. The closet was so stuffed the doors wouldn't shut, and clothes oozed from the set of drawers inside like the stuffing in a hamburger. The curtain rail over the bay window was hung with so many clothes that there was no need for a curtain. The floor and bed were covered in baskets and bags filled with magazines and papers. When my client came home from work, she moved the things on her bed to the floor and when she woke up, she put them back on the bed to make a path to the door so she could go to work. Her lifestyle could not have been called "feminine" by any stretch of the imagination.

"What do you mean by a 'feminine lifestyle'?" I asked. She thought for a long moment before finally responding.

"Well, when I come home from work, the floor would be clear of clutter . . . and my room, as tidy as a hotel suite with nothing obstructing the line of sight. I'd have a pink bedspread and a white antique-style lamp. Before going to bed, I would have a bath, burn aromatherapy oils, and listen to classical piano or violin while doing yoga and drinking herbal tea. I would fall asleep with a feeling of unhurried spaciousness."

Her description was as vivid as if she actually lived that way. It's important to achieve this degree of concreteness when visualizing your ideal lifestyle. If you find that hard, if you can't picture the kind of life you would like to have, try looking in interior decorating magazines for photos that grab you. Visiting model homes can also be useful. Seeing a variety of homes will help you get a feel for what you like. By the way, the client I described above does indeed enjoy post-bath aromatherapy, classical music, and yoga. Redeemed from the depths of disorder, she emerged to grasp the "feminine lifestyle" to which she aspired.

Now that you can picture the lifestyle you dream of, is it time to move on to discarding? No, not yet. I can understand your impatience, but to prevent rebound you need to move ahead properly, step by step, as you launch into this once-in-a-lifetime event. Your next step is to identify *why* you want to live like that. Look back over your notes about the kind of lifestyle you want, and think again. Why do you want to do aromatherapy before bed? Why do you want to listen to classical music while doing yoga? If the answers are "because I want to relax before bed," and "I want to do yoga to lose weight," ask yourself why you want to relax and why you want to lose weight. Maybe your answers will be "I don't want to be tired when I go to work the next day," and "I want to lose weight so that I can be more svelte." Ask yourself "Why?" again, for each answer. Repeat this process three to five times for every item.

As you continue to explore the reasons behind your ideal lifestyle, you will come to a simple realization. The whole point in both discarding and keeping things is to be happy. It may seem obvious, but it is important to experience this realization for yourself and let it sink into your heart. Before you start tidying, look at the lifestyle you aspire to and ask yourself, "Why do I want to tidy?" When you find the answer, you are ready to move on to the next step: examining what you own.

Selection criterion: does it spark joy?

What standard do you use to decide what to get rid of?

There are several common patterns when it comes to discarding. One is to discard things when they cease being functional—for example, when something breaks down beyond repair or when part of a set is broken. Another is to discard things that are out of date, such as clothes that are no longer in fashion or things related to an event that has passed. It's easy to get rid of things when there is an obvious reason for doing so. It's much more difficult when there is no compelling reason. Various experts have proposed yardsticks for discarding things people find hard to part with. These include such rules as "discard anything you haven't used for a year," and "if you can't decide, pack those items away in a box and look at them again six months later." **However, the moment you start focusing on *how* to choose what to throw away, you have actually veered significantly off course.** In this state, it is extremely risky to continue tidying.

At one point in my life, I was virtually a "disposal unit." After discovering *The Art of Discarding* when I was fifteen, I focused on how to get rid of things, and my research efforts escalated. I was always looking for new places to practice, be it my siblings' rooms or the communal storage lockers at school. My head was full of tidying tips, and I had complete, albeit misguided, confidence that I could tidy any place.

My particular goal at that time was to get rid of as much as possible. I applied every criteria suggested by the various books I read on reducing. I tried getting rid of clothes that I hadn't worn for two years, discarding another item every time I bought something new, and throwing away anything I wasn't sure of. I threw out thirty bags of garbage in one month. But no matter how much I discarded, not a single room in my house felt any tidier.

In fact, I found myself going shopping just to relieve the stress and so failed miserably to reduce the total volume of my possessions. At home, I was always uptight, constantly on the lookout for superfluous things that could be discarded. When I found something not in use, I would pounce on it vengefully and throw it in the garbage. Not surprisingly, I became increasingly irritable and tense and found it impossible to relax even in my own home.

One day after school, I opened the door to my room to begin cleaning as usual. At the sight of that untidy space, I finally lost it. "I don't want to tidy anymore!" I cried. Plopping myself down in the middle of my room, I began to think. I had spent three years tidying and discarding things, yet my room still felt cluttered. *Would someone please tell me why my room isn't tidy when I work so hard at it?* Although I did not say this out loud, in my heart I was practically shouting. At that moment, I heard a voice.

"Look more closely at what is there."

What do you mean? I look at what's here so closely every day I could drill a hole through it all. With that thought still in my head, I fell fast asleep right there on the floor. If I had been a little smarter, I would have realized before I became so neurotic that focusing solely on throwing things away can only bring unhappiness. Why? Because **we should be choosing what we want to keep, not what we want to get rid of.**

When I woke up, I knew immediately what that voice in my head had meant. *Look more closely at what is there.* I had been so focused on what to discard, on attacking the unwanted obstacles around me, that I had forgotten to cherish the things that I loved, the things I wanted to keep. Through this experience, I came to the conclusion that the best way to choose what to keep and what to throw away is to **take each item in one's hand and ask: "Does this spark joy?" If it does, keep it. If not, dispose of it.** This is not only the simplest but also the most accurate yardstick by which to judge.

You may wonder about the effectiveness of such a vague criteria, but the trick is to handle each item. Don't just open up your closet and decide after a cursory glance that everything in it gives you a thrill. You must take each outfit in your hand. When you touch a piece of clothing, your body reacts. Its response to each item is different. Trust me and try it.

I chose this standard for a reason. After all, what is the point in tidying? If it's not so that our space and the things in it can bring us happiness, then I think there is no point at all. Therefore, the best criterion for choosing what to keep and what to discard is whether keeping it will make you happy, whether it will bring you joy.

Are you happy wearing clothes that don't give you pleasure?

Do you feel joy when surrounded by piles of unread books that don't touch your heart?

Do you think that owning accessories you know you'll never use will ever bring you happiness?

The answer to these questions should be no.

Now imagine yourself living in a space that contains only things that spark joy. Isn't this the lifestyle you dream of?

Keep only those things that speak to your heart. Then take the plunge and discard all the rest. By doing this, you can reset your life and embark on a new lifestyle.

One category at a time

Deciding what to keep on the basis of what sparks joy in your heart is the most important step in tidying. But what concrete steps are needed to efficiently eliminate excess?

Let me begin by telling you what not to do. Don't start selecting and discarding by location. Don't think "I'll tidy the bedroom first and then move on to the living room" or "I'll go through my drawers one by one starting from the top down." This approach is fatal. Why? Because most people don't bother to store similar items in the same place.

In the majority of households, items that fall into the same category are stored in two or more places scattered around the house. Say, for example, you start with the bedroom closet. After you have finished sorting and discarding everything in it, you are bound to come across clothes you kept in a different closet or a coat draped over a living room chair. You will then have to repeat the whole process of choosing and storing, wasting time and effort, and you cannot make an accurate assessment of what you want to keep and discard under such conditions. Repetition and wasted effort can kill motivation, and therefore it must be avoided.

For this reason, I recommend that you **always think in terms of category, not place**. Before choosing what to keep, collect everything that falls within the same category at one time. Take every last item out and lay everything in one spot. To demonstrate the steps involved, let's go back to the example of clothing above. You start by deciding that you are going to organize and put away your clothes. The next step is to search every room of the house. Bring every piece of clothing you find to the same place, and spread them out on the floor. Then pick up each outfit and see if it sparks joy. Those and only those are the ones to keep. Follow this procedure for every category. If you have too many clothes, you can make subcategories such as tops, bottoms, socks, and so on, and examine your clothes, one subcategory at a time.

Gathering every item in one place is essential to this process because it gives you an accurate grasp of how much you have. Most people are shocked at the sheer volume, which is often at least twice what they imagined. By collecting things in one spot, you can also compare items that are similar in design, making it easier to decide whether you want to keep them.

I have another good reason for removing all items in the same category from drawers, closets, and cupboards and spreading them out on the floor. Things stored out of sight are dormant. This makes it much harder to decide whether they inspire joy or not. By exposing them to the light of day and jolting them alive, so to speak, you'll find it's surprisingly easy to judge whether they touch your heart.

Dealing with just one category within a single time frame speeds up the tidying process. So be sure to gather every item in the category you are working on. Don't let any slip by unnoticed.

Starting with mementos spells certain failure

You launch into your day all fired up to tidy, but before you know it the sun is setting and you've barely made a dent in your belongings. Noticing the time with a start, you feel yourself sinking into self-reproach and despair. And what are you holding in your hands? More often than not, it's one of your favorite comic books, an album, or some other item that brings back fond memories.

My advice to begin tidying not by room but by category does not mean that you should start with any category you like. The degree of difficulty involved in selecting what to keep and what to discard differs greatly depending on the category. People who get stuck halfway usually do so because they start with the things that are hardest to make decisions about. Things that bring back memories, such as photos, are not the place for beginners to start. Not only is the sheer volume of items in this category usually greater than that of any other, but it is also far harder to make a decision about whether or not to keep them.

In addition to the physical value of things, there are three other factors that add value to our belongings: function, information, and emotional attachment. When the element of rarity is added, the difficulty in choosing what to discard multiplies. **People have trouble discarding things that they could still use (functional value), that contain helpful information (informational value), and that have sentimental ties (emotional value). When these things are hard to obtain or replace (rarity), they become even harder to part with.**

The process of deciding what to keep and what to discard will go much more smoothly if you begin with items that are easier to make decisions about. As you gradually work toward the harder categories, you will be honing your decision-making skills. Clothes are the easiest because their rarity value is extremely low. Photographs and letters, on the other hand, not only have a high sentimental value but also are one of a kind; therefore, they should be left until last. This is true for photographs, in particular, because they tend to turn up at random while sorting through other categories and in the most unexpected places, such as between books and papers. **The best sequence is this: clothes first, then books, papers, *komono* (miscellany), and lastly, mementos.** This order has also proven to be the most efficient in terms of the level of difficulty for the subsequent task of storing. Finally, sticking to this sequence sharpens our intuitive sense of what items spark joy inside us. If you can dramatically accelerate the speed of the decision-making process just by changing the order in which you discard, don't you think it's worth a try?

Don't let your family see

Marathon tidying produces a heap of garbage. At this stage, the one disaster that can wreak more havoc than an earthquake is the entrance of that recycling expert who goes by the alias of "mother."

One of my clients, whom I'll call "M," lived with her parents and one sibling. They had moved to the house fifteen years earlier when M was still in grade school. Not only did she love buying clothes, but she also saved those that had sentimental value, such as school uniforms and T-shirts made for various events. She stored these in boxes and stacked them on the floor until the floorboards were completely obscured from view. It took five hours to sort and clean. By the end of that day, she had fifteen bags to get rid of, including eight bags of clothes, two hundred books, various stuffed toys, and crafts she had made at school. We had stacked everything neatly beside the door on the floor, which was now finally visible, and I was just about to explain a very important point.

"There's one secret you should know about getting rid of this garbage," I began, when the door opened and in came her mother bearing a tray of iced tea. *Oh dear,* I thought.

Her mother set down the tray on a table. "Thank you so much for helping my daughter," she said and turned to leave. At that moment, her eyes fell on the pile of garbage by the door. "Oh my, are you going to throw that away?" she said, pointing to a pink yoga mat on top of the pile.

"I haven't used it in two years."

"Really? Well, maybe I'll use it then." She began rummaging through the bags. "Oh, and maybe this, too." When she left, she took not only the yoga mat but also three skirts, two blouses, two jackets, and some stationery.

When the room was quiet again, I sipped my iced tea and asked M, "So how often does your mother do yoga?"

"I've never seen her do any."

What I had been about to say before her mother came in was this. "Don't let your family see what's here. If at all possible, take the bags out yourself. There's no need to let your family know the details of what you throw out or donate."

I especially recommend that my clients avoid showing their parents. It's not that there is anything to be ashamed of. There's nothing wrong with tidying. However, **it's extremely stressful for parents to see what their children discard.** The sheer volume of the pile can make parents anxious about whether their children can survive on what's left. In addition, despite knowing that they should rejoice at their child's independence and maturity, parents can find it very painful to see clothes, toys, and mementos from the past on the rubbish heap, especially if they are things they gave to their child. Keeping your garbage out of sight is considerate. It also protects your family from acquiring more than they need or can enjoy. Up to this point, your family was perfectly content with what they had. When they see what you have chosen to discard, they may feel guilty at such blatant waste, but the items they retrieve from your pile just increase the burden of unnecessary items in their home. And we *should* be ashamed of forcing them to carry this burden.

In an overwhelming percentage of cases, it is the mother who retrieves things from her daughter, yet mothers rarely wear the clothes they take. The women

I work with who are in their fifties and sixties invariably end up discarding or donating their daughters' hand-me-downs without ever wearing them. I think we should avoid creating situations like this where a mother's affection for her daughter becomes a burden. Of course, there's nothing wrong with other family members actually using the things you don't need. If you live with your family, you could ask them, "Is there something you need that you were planning to buy?" before you start tidying, and then if you happen to come across exactly what they need, give it to them as a gift.

If you're mad at your family, your room may be the cause

"Even if I tidy, the rest of my family just messes things up again."

"My husband's a packrat. How can I get him to throw things away?"

It can be very annoying when your family doesn't cooperate with your attempts to achieve the "ideal" home. This is something I experienced many times in the past. At one time, I was so absorbed in tidying that cleaning my own room was not enough. I just had to tackle my siblings' rooms and every other space in the house. And I was constantly frustrated by my untidy family. A major cause of distress was the communal storage closet in the middle of the house. To me more than half of it seemed to be devoted to unused and unnecessary junk. The clothing rods were jammed with outfits I had never seen my mother wear and suits belonging to my father that were clearly obsolete. Boxes of manga belonging to my brother covered the floor.

I would wait until the timing was right and confront the owner with this question: "You don't use this anymore, right?" But the response was either, "Yes, I do," or, "I'll get rid of it myself," which they never did. Every time I looked in that closet I would sigh and complain, "Why does everyone keep accumulating things? Can't they see how hard I'm working to keep the house tidy?"

Fully aware that I was an anomaly when it came to tidying, I was not going to let them defeat me. When my frustration reached the limit, I decided to adopt stealth tactics. I identified items that had not been used for many years, judging by their design, the amount of dust they had gathered, and the way they smelled. I would move those items to the very back of the closet and observe what happened. If no one noticed that they were missing, I disposed of them, one item at a time, just as if I were thinning plants. After three months of this strategy, I had managed to dispose of ten bags' worth.

In most cases, no one noticed, and life went on as usual. But when the volume reached a certain point, people began to miss a thing or two. When they pointed the finger at me, I responded quite shamelessly. My basic strategy was to play ignorant.

"Hey, do you know where my jacket went?"

"Nope."

If they pressed me further, my next step was denial.

"Mari, are you sure you didn't throw it out?"

"Yes, I'm sure."

"Oh. Well, I wonder where it could be, then."

If they gave up at this point, my conclusion was that whatever the item had been, it hadn't been worth saving. But if they were no longer fooled, I still wasn't fazed.

"I know it was here, Mari. I saw it with my own eyes just two months ago."

Far from apologizing for discarding their things without permission, I would retort, "I threw it out for you because you weren't capable of doing it yourself."

In retrospect, I must admit that I was pretty arrogant. Once exposed, I was met with a flood of reproach and protest, and, in the end, I was forbidden to tidy anywhere but my own room. If I could, I'd go back and give myself a good smack and make sure that I didn't even consider such a ridiculous campaign. Getting rid of other people's things without permission demonstrates a sad lack of common sense. Although such stealth tactics generally succeed and the items discarded are never missed, the risk of losing your family's trust when you are caught is far too great. Besides, it just isn't right. If you really want your family to tidy up, there is a much easier way to go about it.

After I was banned from tidying other people's spaces and had nowhere to turn but my own room, I took a good look around it and was struck by a surprising fact. There were far more items that needed discarding than I had noticed before—a shirt in my closet that I had never worn along with an outdated skirt that I wouldn't wear again, books on my shelves that I knew I didn't need. I realized with a shock that I was guilty of exactly the same thing I had been so bitterly accusing my family of doing. Not being in a position to criticize others, I sat down with my garbage bags and focused on tidying my own space.

After about two weeks, a change began to occur in my family. My brother, who had refused, no matter how much I had complained, to get rid of anything, began a thorough sorting of his belongings. In a single day, he disposed of more than two hundred books. Then my parents and my sister gradually began to sort and discard their clothes and accessories. In the end, my whole family was able to keep the house much tidier than before.

To quietly work away at disposing of your own excess is actually the best way of dealing with a family that doesn't tidy. As if drawn into your wake, they will begin weeding out unnecessary belongings and tidying without your having to utter a single complaint. It may sound incredible, but when someone starts tidying it sets off a chain reaction.

Cleaning quietly on one's own generates another interesting change—the ability to tolerate a certain level of untidiness among your family members. Once I was satisfied with my own room, I no longer felt the urge to dispose of things belonging to my siblings or parents. When I noticed that communal spaces such as the living room or bathroom were messy, I cleaned them up without a second thought and never bothered to mention it. I have noticed this same change occur in many of my clients as well.

If you feel annoyed with your family for being untidy, I urge you to check your own space, especially your storage. You are bound to find things that need to be thrown away. **The urge to point out someone else's failure to tidy is usually a sign that you are neglecting to take care of your own space.** This is why you should begin by discarding only your own things. You can leave the communal spaces to the end. The first step is to confront your own stuff.

What you don't need, your family doesn't either

My sister is three years younger than me. Quiet and a bit on the shy side, she prefers to stay inside and draw or read quietly rather than to go out and socialize. Without a doubt, she suffered the most from my research on tidying, serving as my unsuspecting victim. By the time I was a university student, my focus was on "discarding," but there were always things that I found hard to dispose of, such as a T-shirt that I really liked but that somehow didn't look right. Unable to bring myself to part with it, I would try the item on repeatedly, standing in front of the mirror, but in the end, would be forced to conclude that it just didn't suit me. If it was brand new, or a gift from my parents, the thought of getting rid of it made me feel very guilty.

At times like this, my sister came in very handy. The "gift for my sister" method seemed the perfect way to cast off such items. When I say "gift," I don't mean that I wrapped it up like a present—far from it. With the unwanted outfit in my hand, I would barge into my sister's room where she lay on her bed reading contentedly. Extracting the book from her hand, I would say, "You want this T-shirt? I'll give it to you if you like." Seeing the puzzled look on her face, I would deal the final blow. "It's brand new and really cute. But if you don't need it, I'll have to throw it away. Are you OK with that?"

My poor, mild-mannered sister would have no choice but to say, "I guess I'll take it then."

This happened so frequently that my sister, who hardly ever shopped, had a closet jammed to overflowing. Although she did wear some of the clothes I gave her, there were many more that she wore only once if ever. Yet I continued to give her "presents." After all, they were good clothes and I thought she should be happy to have more. I only realized how wrong I was after I began my consulting business and met a client whom I will call "K."

K was in her twenties, worked for a cosmetics company, and lived at home. As we were sorting through her clothes, I began to notice something odd about the choices she was making. Despite the fact that she owned enough clothes to fill one large closet, which is an average-size wardrobe, the number of clothes she chose to keep seemed unnaturally small. Her answer to the question, "Does this spark joy?" was almost always "No." After thanking each item for a job well done, I would pass them to her to discard. I couldn't help noticing the look of relief on her face every time she put an outfit in the bag. Examining the collection more closely, I saw that the clothes she chose to keep were mostly casual things like T-shirts, while the ones she discarded were a completely different style— tight skirts and revealing tops. When I asked her about this, she said, "My older sister gave me those." When all the clothes were sorted and she had made her final choice, she murmured, "Look at that. I was surrounded by all this stuff that I didn't even like." Her sister's hand-me-downs had comprised over a third of her wardrobe, but hardly any of these had given her that important thrill of pleasure. Although she had worn them because her sister had given them to her, she had never liked them.

To me, this seems tragic. And this is not an isolated case. In my work, the volume discarded by younger sisters is always greater than the volume discarded by older sisters, a phenomenon surely related to the fact that younger children are often accustomed to wearing hand-me-downs. There are two reasons why younger sisters tend to collect clothes they don't really like. One is that it's hard to get rid of something received from family. The other is that they don't really know what they like, which makes it hard to decide whether they should part with it. Because they receive so much clothing from others, they don't really need to shop and therefore they have less opportunity to develop the instinct for what really inspires joy.

Don't misunderstand me. Giving things you can't use to others who can is an excellent idea. Not only is it economical, but it can also be a source of great joy to see these things being enjoyed and treasured by someone close to you. But that is not the same as forcing things onto your family members because you can't bring yourself to discard or donate them. Whether the victim is a sibling, a parent, or a child, this particular custom should be banned. Although my sister never complained, I am sure that she must have had mixed feelings when she accepted my hand-me-downs. Basically, I was simply transferring my guilt at not being able to discard them onto her. In retrospect, that was pretty despicable.

If you want to give something away, don't push people to take it unconditionally or pressure them by making them feel guilty. Find out in advance what they like, and if you find something that fits those criteria, then and only then should you show it to them. You can also offer to give it to them on the condition that it is something they would have been willing to pay for. We need to show consideration for others by helping them avoid the burden of owning more than they need or can enjoy.

Tidying is a dialogue with one's self

"KonMari, would you like to come stand under a waterfall?"

I got this invitation from a client, a charming woman who was still an active business manager and an avid skier and hiker at the age of seventy-four. She had been practicing meditation under running water for more than a decade and seemed to really enjoy it. She would casually remark, "I'm off to a waterfall," as if she were going to the spa. Consequently, the place she took me was not a spot for beginners on an introductory tour. Leaving our lodgings at six in the morning, we hiked along a mountain path, climbed over fences, and forded a river where the rushing water came up to our knees, until we finally reached a deserted waterfall.

But I didn't bring up this subject because I wanted to introduce this peculiar form of recreation. Rather, I found through this experience that there is significant similarity between meditating under a waterfall and tidying. When you stand under a waterfall, the only audible sound is the roar of water. As the cascade pummels your body, the sensation of pain soon disappears and numbness spreads. Then a sensation of heat warms you from the inside out, and you enter a meditative trance. Although I had never tried this form of meditation before, the sensation it generated seemed extremely familiar. It closely resembled what I experience when I am tidying. While not exactly a meditative state, there are times when I am cleaning that I can quietly commune with myself. The work of carefully considering each object I own to see whether it sparks joy inside me is like conversing with myself through the medium of my possessions.

For this reason, it is essential to create a quiet space in which to evaluate the things in your life. Ideally, you should not even be listening to music. Sometimes I hear of methods that recommend tidying in time to a catchy song, but personally, I don't encourage this. I feel that noise makes it harder to hear the internal dialogue between the owner and his or her belongings. Listening to the TV is, of course, out of the question. If you need some background noise to relax, choose environmental or ambient music with no lyrics or well-defined melodies. If you want to add momentum to your tidying work, tap the power of the atmosphere in your room rather than relying on music.

The best time to start is early morning. The fresh morning air keeps your mind clear and your power of discernment sharp. For this reason, most of my lessons commence in the morning. The earliest lesson I ever conducted began at six thirty, and we were able to clean at twice the usual speed.

The clear, refreshed feeling gained after standing under a waterfall can be addictive. Similarly, when you finish putting your space in order, you will be overcome with the urge to do it again. And, unlike waterfall meditation, you don't have to travel long distances over hard terrain to get there. You can enjoy the same effect in your own home. That's pretty special, don't you think?

What to do when you can't throw something away

My criterion for deciding to keep an item is that we should feel a thrill of joy when we touch it. But it is human nature to resist throwing something away even when we know that we should. Items that we can't bring ourselves to discard even when they don't inspire joy are a real problem.

Human judgment can be divided into two broad types: intuitive and rational. When it comes to selecting what to discard, it is actually our rational judgment that causes trouble. Although intuitively we know that an object has no attraction for us, our reason raises all kinds of arguments for not discarding it, such as "I might need it later" or "It's a waste to get rid of it." These thoughts spin round and round in our mind, making it impossible to let go.

I am not claiming that it is wrong to hesitate. The inability to decide demonstrates a certain degree of attachment to a particular object. Nor can all decisions be made on intuition alone. But this is precisely why we need to consider each object with care and not be distracted by thoughts of being wasteful.

When you come across something that's hard to discard, consider carefully why you have that specific item in the first place. When did you get it and what meaning did it have for you then? Reassess the role it plays in your life. If, for example, you have some clothes that you bought but never wear, examine them one at a time. Where did you buy that particular outfit and why? If you bought it because you thought it looked cool in the shop, it has fulfilled the function of giving you a thrill when you bought it. Then why did you never wear it? Was it because you realized that it didn't suit you when you tried it on at home? If so, and if you no longer buy clothes of the same style or color, it has fulfilled another important function—it has taught you what doesn't suit you. In fact, that particular article of clothing has already completed its role in your life, and you are free to say, "Thank you for giving me joy when I bought you," or "Thank you for teaching me what doesn't suit me," and let it go.

Every object has a different role to play. Not all clothes have come to you to be worn threadbare. It is the same with people. Not every person you meet in life will become a close friend or lover. Some you will find hard to get along with or impossible to like. But these people, too, teach you the precious lesson of who you *do* like, so that you will appreciate those special people even more.

When you come across something that you cannot part with, think carefully about its true purpose in your life. You'll be surprised at how many of the things you possess have already fulfilled their role. By acknowledging their contribution and letting them go with gratitude, you will be able to truly put the things you own, and your life, in order. In the end, all that will remain are the things that you really treasure.

To truly cherish the things that are important to you, you must first discard those that have outlived their purpose. To get rid of what you no longer need is neither wasteful nor shameful. Can you truthfully say that you treasure something buried so deeply in a closet or drawer that you have forgotten its existence? If things had feelings, they would certainly not be happy. Free them from the prison to which you have relegated them. Help them leave that deserted isle to which you have exiled them. Let them go, with gratitude. Not only you, but your things as well, will feel clear and refreshed when you are done tidying.

3

—

Tidying by category works like magic

Tidying order

Follow the correct order of categories

The door opens with a click, and a woman looks out at me somewhat anxiously. "H-hello." My clients almost always seem a bit tense the first time I visit their home. As they have already met me several times, this tenseness stems not from shyness but more from the need to brace themselves for a major challenge.

"Do you think it's really possible to clean up my house? There's no place to even put your feet in here."

"I don't see how I can really tidy completely in such a short time."

"You said that none of your clients have ever suffered rebound. But what if I'm the first?"

Their nervous excitement is almost palpable, but I know without a doubt that every one of them will do fine. Even those who are lazy or messy by nature, even people who have descended from generations of slobs or who are excessively busy, can learn to clean properly if they use the KonMari Method.

Let me share a secret. Putting your house in order is fun! The process of assessing how you feel about the things you own, identifying those that have fulfilled their purpose, expressing your gratitude, and bidding them farewell, is really about examining your inner self, a rite of passage to a new life. The yardstick by which you judge is your intuitive sense of attraction, and therefore there's no need for complex theories or numerical data. All you need to do is follow the right order. So arm yourself with plenty of garbage bags and prepare to have fun.

Start with clothes, then move on to books, papers, *komono* (miscellany), and finally things with sentimental value. If you reduce what you own in this order, your work will proceed with surprising ease. By starting with the easy things first and leaving the hardest for last, you can gradually hone your decision-making skills, so that by the end, it seems simple.

For the first category, clothing, I recommend dividing further into the following subcategories to increase efficiency:

Tops (shirts, sweaters, etc.)

Bottoms (pants, skirts, etc.)

Clothes that should be hung (jackets, coats, suits, etc.)

Socks

Underwear

Bags (handbags, messenger bags, etc.)

Accessories (scarves, belts, hats, etc.)

Clothes for specific events (swimsuits, kimonos, uniforms, etc.)

Shoes

And, yes, I include handbags and shoes as clothing.

Why is this the optimal order? I am actually not sure why, but based on the experience I've gained devoting half my life to tidying, I can tell you for certain that it works! Believe me. If you follow this order, you'll speed through the work and achieve visible results surprisingly quickly. Moreover, because you will keep only the things you truly love, your energy and joy will increase. You may be physically tired, but it feels so good to get rid of unnecessary items that you will find it hard to stop.

The important point, however, is deciding what to keep. **What things will bring you joy if you keep them as part of your life?** Pick them as if you were identifying items you loved from a showcase in your favorite store. Once you've grasped the basics, put all your clothes in one heap, take them in your hand one by one, and ask yourself quietly, "Does this spark joy?" Your tidying festival has begun.

Clothing

Place every item of clothing in the house on the floor

The first step is to check every closet and dresser in the house and gather all your clothes in one spot. Don't leave a single wardrobe or dresser drawer unopened. Make sure you have gathered every last piece of clothing. When my clients think they have finished, I always ask them this question. "Are you sure there's not a single piece of clothing left in the house?" Then I add, "You can forget about any clothes you find after this. They'll automatically go in the discard pile." I let them know I'm quite serious. I have no intention of letting them keep anything found after the sorting is done. The response is usually, "Oh, wait. I think there might be something in my husband's closet," or "Ah! I might have hung something in the hallway," followed by one last dash around the house and a few extra items added to the pile.

This ultimatum sounds a bit like the automatic withdrawal system for paying bills at the bank, but when my clients know there's a firm deadline, they search their memories one more time because they don't want to lose clothes without being given a chance to decide. Although I rarely have to follow through on my threat, if someone doesn't remember an item at this point, it obviously doesn't inspire a thrill of joy, and therefore I am quite ruthless. The only exception is clothes that happen to be in the laundry.

When all the clothes have been gathered together, the pile of tops alone is usually knee-deep. The term "tops" includes clothes for every season, from T-shirts and camisoles to knitted sweaters. The average number of items in this initial pile is around 160. Confronted by their first obstacle in the tidying process, most people are overwhelmed by the sheer volume of what they actually own. At this point, I usually say, "Let's start with off-season clothes." I have a good reason for choosing off-season clothing for their first foray into this tidying gala. It's the easiest category for tuning in to one's intuition concerning what feels good.

If they start with clothes they are currently using, clients are more likely to think, "It doesn't spark joy, but I just wore it yesterday," or "If I don't have any clothes left to wear, what am I going to do?" This makes it harder for them to make an objective decision. Because off-season clothes are not imminently necessary, it is much easier to apply the simple criterion of whether or not they bring you joy. There's one question I recommend asking when you select off-season clothes. "Do I want to see this outfit again next time it's in season?" Or, to rephrase it, "Would I want to wear this right away if the temperature suddenly changed?"

"Do I want to see it again? Well, not necessarily. . . ." If that's how you feel, throw it in the discard or donate pile. And if you got a lot of wear out of it last season, don't forget to express your appreciation. You might fear that you'll have no clothes left if you use this standard. But don't worry. It may seem as if you have discarded an awful lot, but as long as you are choosing clothes that give you pleasure, you'll be left with the amount you need.

Once you have gotten the knack of choosing what you love, you can move on to each subcategory of in-season clothing. **The most important points to remember are** these: Make sure you gather every piece of clothing in the house and be sure to handle each one.

Loungewear
Downgrading to "loungewear" is taboo

It seems a waste to get rid of something that is still perfectly usable, especially if you bought it yourself. In cases like this, my clients often ask me if they can keep clothes they know they'll never wear outside and use them as loungewear. If I said "yes," the pile of loungewear would grow ever larger without any decrease in the overall volume of clothes.

Having said that, I admit that I myself once did the same thing with clothes I knew I'd never wear to go out. Pilled cardigans, outdated blouses, dresses that didn't suit me or that I just never wore—it wasn't long before I had developed the habit of demoting clothes like these to "loungewear" rather than discarding them. Yet nine out of ten times I never wore them.

I soon discovered that many of my clients also had collections of dormant "loungewear." When asked why they don't wear them, their answers are very revealing: "I can't relax in them," "It seems a waste to wear this inside when it was really for going out," "I don't like it," and so on. In other words, these castoffs are not really loungewear at all.

Calling them that merely delays parting with clothes that don't spark any joy. There are stores dedicated solely to loungewear products, and the design, material, and cut are all aimed at relaxation. Obviously, it is a completely different genre from what we wear outside. Cotton T-shirts are probably the only type of regular clothing that could be reused in this category.

To me, it doesn't seem right to keep clothes we don't enjoy for relaxing around the house. This time at home is still a precious part of living. Its value should not change just because nobody sees us. So, starting today, break the habit of downgrading clothes that don't thrill you to loungewear. The real waste is not discarding clothes you don't like but wearing them even though you are striving to create the ideal space for your ideal lifestyle. Precisely because no one is there to see you, it makes far more sense to reinforce a positive self-image by wearing clothes you love.

The same goes for pajamas. If you are a woman, try wearing something elegant as nightwear. The worst thing you can do is to wear a sloppy sweat suit. I occasionally meet people who dress like this all the time, whether waking or sleeping. If sweatpants are your everyday attire, you'll end up looking like you belong in them, which is not very attractive. What you wear in the house does impact your self-image.

Clothing storage

Fold it right and solve your storage problems

After the selection process, my clients are usually left with only a third to a quarter of the clothes they started out with. As the clothes they want to keep are still piled in the middle of the floor, it is time to start putting them away. Before I go on to that step, however, let me tell you a story.

I once had a client with a problem that I just could not understand. A woman in her fifties, she told me during our initial interview that she didn't have enough closet space in her house for all her clothes. From the floor plan, however, it was clear not only that she had two full closets to herself but that those closets were one and a half times larger than average. Although this should have been plenty of space, she also had a clothing stand with three rods full of clothes.

Amazed, I roughly estimated that she must have more than two thousand outfits in her wardrobe. It was only when I visited her home that I finally understood. Upon opening her wall-length closet, my jaw dropped. It was like looking at the crowded racks at the dry cleaners. Hanging neatly on hangers were not just coats and skirts but also T-shirts, sweaters, purses, and even underwear.

My client immediately launched into a detailed explanation of her hanger collection. "This type is made especially for knits so that they don't slip off. And these are handmade. I bought them in Germany." After a five-minute lecture, she beamed at me and said, "Clothes don't get wrinkled if you hang them up. And they last longer, too, right?" Upon further questioning, I discovered that she did not fold any of her clothes at all.

There are two storage methods for clothes: one is to put them on hangers and hang from a rod and the other is to fold them and put them away in drawers. I can understand why people might be attracted to hanging their clothes. It seems like far less work. However, I strongly recommend folding as the main storage method. *But it's a pain to fold clothes and put them away in the drawer. It's much easier to pop them on a hanger and stick them in the closet.* If that's what you're thinking, then you haven't discovered the true impact of folding.

Hanging just can't compete with folding for saving space. Although it depends somewhat on the thickness of the clothes in question, you can fit from twenty to forty pieces of folded clothing in the same amount of space required to hang ten. The client described above had only slightly more clothes than average. If she had folded them, she would have had no problem fitting them into her storage space. **By neatly folding your clothes, you can solve almost every problem related to storage.**

But that is not the only effect of folding. The real benefit is that you must handle each piece of clothing. As you run your hands over the cloth, you pour your energy into it. The Japanese word for healing is *te-ate,* which literally means "to apply hands." The term originated prior to the development of modern medicine when people believed that placing one's hand on an injury promoted healing. We know that gentle physical contact from a parent, such as holding hands, patting a child on the head, and hugging, has a calming effect on children. Likewise, a firm but gentle massage by human hands does much more to loosen knotted muscles than being pummeled by a massage machine. The energy that flows from the person's hands into our skin seems to heal both body and soul.

The same is true for clothing. When we take our clothes in our hands and fold them neatly, we are, I believe, transmitting energy, which has a positive effect on our clothes. Folding properly pulls the cloth taut and erases wrinkles, and makes the material stronger and more vibrant. Clothes that have been neatly folded have a resilience and sheen that can be discerned immediately, clearly distinguishing them from those that have been haphazardly stuffed in a drawer. The act of folding is far more than making clothes compact for storage. It is an act of caring, an expression of love and appreciation for the way these clothes support your lifestyle. Therefore, when we fold, we should put our heart into it, thanking our clothes for protecting our bodies.

In addition, folding clothes after they have been washed and dried is an opportunity to really notice them in all their detail. For example, we might spot places where the cloth has frayed or see that a certain piece of clothing is becoming worn out. Folding is really a form of dialogue with our wardrobe. Japanese traditional clothing, kimono and yukata, were always folded into rectangles to fit perfectly into drawers designed to their uniform dimensions. I don't think there is any other culture in the world where storage units and clothing were matched so precisely. Japanese people quickly grasp the pleasure that comes from folding clothes, almost as if they are genetically programmed for this task.

How to fold

The best way to fold for perfect appearance

The laundry is done and ready to be put away, but this is where many people get stuck. Folding seems like extra work, especially as the clothes will be worn again soon anyway. Many people can't be bothered and soon they have a heap of clothes on the floor. They fall into the daily routine of picking something out of the pile to wear while the mound continues to grow, eventually spreading from one corner to take over the rest of the room.

If this describes you, don't worry. None of my clients have ever known how to fold clothes properly when they began taking my lessons. In fact, quite a few of them declared that it was their policy never to fold their clothes. I have opened closets so full that the clothes look like they have been hardened in a jelly mold, and I have witnessed drawers filled with clothes rolled and twisted like noodles. You would think my clients had never seen the first letter of the word "fold." But once they finish my course, all of them, without exception, have told me, "Folding is fun!"

One of my clients, a young woman in her twenties, hated folding so much that her mother used to come and do it for her. Through the course, however, she came to love it and even taught her mother how to fold properly. Once you have mastered this technique, you will actually enjoy doing it every day and will find it a handy skill for the rest of your life. In fact, to go through life without knowing how to fold is a huge loss.

The first step is to visualize what the inside of your drawer will look like when you finish. The goal should be to organize the contents so that you can see where every item is at a glance, just as you can see the spines of the books on your bookshelves. **The key is to store things standing up rather than laid flat.** Some people mimic store displays, folding each piece of clothing into a large square and then arranging them one on top of the other in layers. This is great for temporary sales displays in stores, but not what we should be aiming for at home, where our relationship with these clothes is long term.

To store clothes standing, they must be made compact, which means more folds. Some people believe that more folds means more wrinkles, but this is not the case. It is not the number of folds but rather the amount of pressure applied that causes wrinkling. Even lightly folded clothes will wrinkle if they are stored in a pile because the weight of the clothes acts like a press. Think of the difference between folding one sheet of paper as opposed to a hundred sheets in one go. It is much harder to get a sharp crease when folding a whole stack of paper at one time.

Once you have an image of what the inside of your drawers will look like, you can begin folding. **The goal is to fold each piece of clothing into a simple, smooth rectangle.** First, fold each lengthwise side of the garment toward the center (such as the left-hand, then right-hand, sides of a shirt) and tuck the sleeves in to make a long rectangular shape. It doesn't matter how you fold the sleeves. Next, pick up one short end of the rectangle and fold it toward the other short end. Then fold again, in the same manner, in halves or in thirds. The number of folds should be adjusted so that the folded clothing when standing on edge fits the height of the drawer. This is the basic principle that will ultimately allow your clothes to be stacked on edge, side by side, so that when you pull open your drawer you can see the edge of every item inside. If you find that the end result is the right shape but too loose and floppy to stand up, it's a sign that your way of folding doesn't match the type of clothing. **Every piece of clothing has its own "sweet spot" where it feels just right**—a folded state that best suits that item. This will differ depending on the type of material and size of the clothing, and therefore you will need to adjust your method until you find what works. This isn't difficult. By adjusting the height when folded so that it stands properly, you'll reach the sweet spot surprisingly easily.

Folding goes even more smoothly if you fold thin, soft material more tightly, reducing it to a small width and height, and thick, fluffy materials less. In cases where one end of the piece of clothing is thicker than the other, it also helps to keep the thinner end in your hand while folding. There is nothing more satisfying than finding that "sweet spot." The piece of clothing keeps its shape when stood on edge and feels just right when held in your hand. It's like a sudden revelation—*So this is how you always wanted to be folded!*—a historical moment in which your mind and the piece of clothing connect. I love the way my clients' faces light up at that moment.

Arranging clothes
The secret to energizing your closet

It feels great to open up your closet and see the clothes you love arranged neatly on hangers. But my clients' closets are often such a mess that it takes courage just to open them and, once open, it's impossible to find anything in them.

There are two possible causes. The first is that the closet is simply too full. One of my clients had jammed so many clothes inside that it took her three full minutes to extract a single outfit. The hangers were so closely packed that when, after much grunting and pulling, she finally managed to extract an outfit, the clothes on either side popped out with it like bread from a toaster. I could see why she had not used that closet for several years. This is an extreme example, but it is true that most people store far more than necessary in their closets. This is one reason I recommend folding whatever clothes you can. Of course, there are some types of clothing that are better stored on hangers. These include coats, suits, jackets, skirts, and dresses. My standard is this: hang any clothes that look like they would be happier hung up, such as those made with soft materials that flutter in the breeze or highly tailored cuts, which protest at being folded. These we should hang willingly.

The other cause of a messy closet is lack of knowledge. Many people simply don't know how to organize clothes on hangers. The most basic rule is to hang clothes in the same category side by side, dividing your closet into a jacket section, a suit section, and so on. Clothes, like people, can relax more freely when in the company of others who are very similar in type, and therefore organizing them by category helps them feel more comfortable and secure. You can literally transform your closet just by applying this principle.

Of course, many people insist that even when they organize their clothes by category, it isn't long before their closets are messy again. So let me introduce a secret for maintaining the neatness of closets that you work hard to organize. **Arrange your clothes so that they rise to the right.** Take a moment to draw an arrow rising toward the right and then another descending to the right. You can do this on paper or just trace them in the air. Did you notice that when you draw an arrow rising to the right it makes you feel lighter? Lines that slope up to the right make people feel comfortable. By using this principle when you organize your closet, you can make the contents look far more exciting.

To do so, hang heavy items on the left side of the closet and light items on the right. Heavy items include those with length, those made from heavier material, and those that are dark in color. As you move toward the right side of the closet, the length of the clothing grows shorter, the material thinner, and the color lighter. **By category, coats would be on the far left, followed by dresses, jackets, pants, skirts, and blouses.** This is the basic order, but depending on the trends in your wardrobe, what classifies as "heavy" in each category will differ. Use your intuition to create a balance that makes it appear as if the clothes are sloping up to the right. In addition, organize the clothes within each category from heavy to light. When you stand in front of a closet that has been reorganized so that the clothes rise to the right, you will feel your heart beat faster and the cells in your body buzz with energy. This energy will also be transmitted to your clothes. Even when you close the closet door, your room will feel fresher. Once you have experienced this, you'll never lose the habit of organizing by category.

Some may question whether paying attention to such details can possibly cause such a change, but why waste your time doubting if incorporating this exciting magic into all your storage spaces could keep your room tidy? It will only take you ten minutes to rearrange your closet by category, so trust me and give it a try. But don't forget that you first need to reduce your wardrobe to only those clothes that you really love.

Storing socks

Treat your socks and stockings with respect

Have you ever had the experience where you thought what you were doing was a good thing but later learned that it had hurt someone? At the time, you were totally unconcerned, oblivious to the other person's feelings. This is somewhat similar to the way many of us treat our socks.

I visited the home of a client in her fifties. As always, we started with her clothes. We moved through her wardrobe at a smooth pace, finished the underwear, and were ready to start organizing her socks. But when she pulled open her sock drawer, I could not suppress a gasp. It was full of potato-like lumps that rolled about. She had folded back the tops to form balls and tied her stockings tightly in the middle. I was speechless. Dressed in a crisp white apron, my client smiled at me and said, "It's easy to pick out what I need this way, and it's quite simple to put them away as well, don't you think?" Although I frequently run into this attitude during my lessons, it never fails to astonish me. Let me state here and now: **Never, ever tie up your stockings. Never, ever ball up your socks.**

I pointed to the balled-up socks. "Look at them carefully. This should be a time for them to rest. Do you really think they can get any rest like that?"

That's right. The socks and stockings stored in your drawer are essentially on holiday. They take a brutal beating in their daily work, trapped between your foot and your shoe, enduring pressure and friction to protect your precious feet. The time they spend in your drawer is their only chance to rest. But if they are folded over, balled up, or tied, they are always in a state of tension, their fabric stretched and their elastic pulled. They roll about and bump into each other every time the drawer is opened and closed. Any socks and stockings unfortunate enough to get pushed to the back of the drawer are often forgotten for so long that their elastic stretches beyond recovery. When the owner finally discovers them and puts them on, it will be too late and they will be relegated to the garbage. What treatment could be worse than this?

Let's begin with how to fold your stockings. If you've tied them up, start by undoing the knot! Lay the toes one on top of the other and fold the stocking in half length-wise. Then fold it into thirds, making sure that the toes are inside, not outside, and that the waistband protrudes slightly at the top. Finally, roll the stocking up toward the waistband. If the waistband is on the outside when you finish, you've done it right. Fold knee-high stockings the same way. With thicker material, such as tights, it is easier to roll if you fold them in half rather than in thirds. The point is that the stocking should be firm and stable when you've finished, much like a sushi roll.

When you store the stockings in your drawer, arrange them on end so that the swirl is visible. If you are storing them in plastic drawers, I recommend putting them into a cardboard box first, so that they don't slip and unroll, and putting the box into the drawer. A shoebox is the perfect size for a stocking divider. This method is a win-win solution. It allows you to see how many stockings you have at a single glance, protects your stockings from damage, and keeps them smooth and unwrinkled so that they are easier to put on. And it makes your stockings much happier, too.

Folding socks is even easier. If you've folded back the tops, start by unfolding them. Place one sock on top of the other and follow the same principles as those for folding clothing. For low-cut socks that just cover the feet, fold-ing twice is enough; for ankle socks, three times; for knee socks and over-knee socks, four to six times. You can adjust the number of folds to achieve the height that best suits the drawer. It's easy. Just aim to make a simple rectangle, the key to folding. Store the socks on edge, just as you did for clothing. You'll be amazed at how little space you need compared to your "potato ball days," and you'll notice your socks breathing a sigh of relief at being untied.

When I see high school students wearing high socks that are loose at the top, I long to tell them how to fold their socks properly.

Seasonal clothes

Eliminate the need to store off-season clothes

June in Japan is the rainy season. It is also traditionally the month for *koromogae*, when people change to summer clothes. This is preceded by several weeks of cleaning and packing away winter clothes and bringing out summer clothes. Whenever this time of year approaches, it reminds me that I used to do this, too. For years, however, I have not bothered to put away off-season clothes. The custom of *koromogae* originated in China and was introduced to Japan as a court custom during the Heian period (794–1185 AD). It was only in the late nineteenth century, when workers and students began to wear uniforms, that the custom was introduced in businesses and schools. Companies and schools officially switched to the summer uniform at the beginning of June and to the winter uniform at the beginning of October. In other words, this rule was only applied within organizations, and its extension to the ordinary home was not really necessary.

But like every other Japanese, I, too, was convinced that I had to store and unpack seasonal clothing twice a year in June and October. I spent these two months busily emptying and refilling the contents of closets and drawers. To be honest, I found this custom a nuisance. If a dress I wanted to wear was stored away in a box on the top shelf of the closet, it seemed like far too much trouble to get it down and dig it out. Instead, I would compromise and wear something else. There were some years when I didn't manage to unpack my summer clothes until July, and I would realize that in the meantime I had bought clothes similar to those I already owned. Often as soon as I got out my summer clothes, the weather would suddenly turn cold again.

The custom of storing seasonal clothes is behind the times. With the introduction of air-conditioning and heating, our homes are less subject to the weather outside. It's not uncommon now to see people wearing T-shirts indoors even in winter. So it's time to abandon this custom and keep all our clothes ready to be used year-round, regardless of the season.

My clients love this approach, especially because they can grasp at all times exactly what clothes they have. No difficult techniques are required. All you need to do is organize your clothes on the premise that you aren't going to put off-season clothes in storage. **The trick is** not to overcategorize. **Divide your clothes roughly into "cotton-like" and "wool-like" materials when you put them in the drawer.** Categorizing by season—summer, winter, fall-and-spring—or by activity, such as work and leisure, should be avoided because it is too vague. If my client's space is limited, I have them store only small, specific off-season items, such as bathing suits and sun hats for the summer season, and mufflers, mittens, and earmuffs for the winter season. Although not a small item, winter coats can also be put away in the back of the closet during the off-season.

For those of you who still don't have enough space, let me share a few tips for storing your off-season clothes. Many people store their off-season clothes in plastic cases with lids. These, however, are the hardest type of storage units to use effectively. Once in the closet, something is bound to be placed on top of it, and pulling the case out and opening it up seems like too much extra work. In the end, it is all too easy to forget the case is even there until the season is almost over. **If you are planning to buy storage units in the near future, I recommend that you get a set of drawers instead.** Be careful not to bury clothes in the cupboard even if they are off-season. Clothes that have been shut up for half a year look wilted, as if they have been stifled. Instead, let in some light and air occasionally. Open the drawer and run your hands over the contents. Let them know you care and look forward to wearing them when they are next in season. This kind of "communication" helps your clothes stay vibrant and keeps your relationship with them alive longer.

Storing books

Put all your books on the floor

Once you have finished organizing and storing your clothes, it's time to move on to books. Books are one of three things that people find hardest to let go. Many people say that books are one thing they just can't part with regardless of whether they are avid readers or not, but the real problem is actually the way in which they part with them.

One of my clients, a woman in her thirties who worked for a foreign consulting firm, loved books. She had read not only every business book but also a broad range of novels and manga. Naturally, her room was filled with books. She had three large ceiling-height bookshelves full of books, plus about twenty waist-high towers of books piled precariously on the floor. When walking through the room, I had to sidestep and twist to avoid bumping into them.

I said to her what I say to all my clients. "Please start by removing every book from your shelves and putting them all on the floor."

Her eyes grew round. "All of them? There's an awful lot."

"Yes, I know. All of them, please."

"But . . ." She hesitated for a moment as though searching for words before continuing. "Wouldn't it be easier to choose them while they're still on the shelf and I can see the titles?"

Books are usually arranged in rows in bookcases so that their titles are clearly visible, so it does seem to make more sense to weed out those you don't want when you can see them. Not only that, but books are heavy. Taking them all off the shelf only to put them back on again seems like a waste of effort. Even so, do not skip this step. Remove all the books from your bookcases. You cannot judge whether or not a book really grabs you when it's still on the shelf. Like clothes or any other belongings, books that have been left untouched on the shelf for a long time are dormant. Or perhaps I should say they're "invisible." Although in plain sight, they remain unseen, just like a praying mantis still in the grass, merging with its surroundings. (Have you ever experienced that jolt of surprise when you suddenly notice it there?)

If you ask yourself, "Does this spark joy?" when you are just looking at the things on your shelves or in your drawers, the question won't mean much to you. To truly decide whether you want to keep something or to dispose of it, you must take your things out of hibernation. Even the piles of books already on the floor will be easier to assess if you move them to a different part of the floor or restack them. Just like the gentle shake we use to wake someone up, we can stimulate our belongings by physically moving them, exposing them to fresh air and making them "conscious."

While helping my clients tidy their homes or offices, I stand in front of the mound of books they have piled on the floor and clap my hands, or I gently stroke the book covers. Although my clients look at me strangely at first, they are inevitably surprised at how quickly and precisely they are able to choose after this. They can see exactly what they need and don't need. It is much harder to choose books when they are still on the shelf, which means you will have to repeat the process later. If there are too many books to arrange on the floor all at one time, I ask my clients to divide them into four broad categories:

General (books you read for pleasure)

Practical (references, cookbooks, etc.)

Visual (photograph collections, etc.)

Magazines

Once you have piled your books, take them in your hand one by one and decide whether you want to keep or discard each one. **The criterion is, of course, whether or not it gives you a thrill of pleasure when you touch it.** Remember, I said when you *touch* it. Make sure you don't start reading it. Reading clouds your judgment. Instead of asking yourself what you feel, you'll start asking whether you need that book or not. Imagine what it would be like to have a bookshelf filled only with books that you really love. Isn't that image spellbinding? For someone who loves books, what greater happiness could there be?

Unread books

"Sometime" means "never"

The most common reason for not discarding a book is "I might read it again." Take a moment to count the number of favorite books that you have actually read more than once. How many are there? For some it may be as few as five while for some exceptional readers it may be as many as one hundred. People who reread that many, however, are usually people in specific professions, such as scholars and authors. Very rarely will you find ordinary people like me who read so many books. Let's face it. **In the end, you are going to read very few of your books again.** As with clothing, we need to stop and think about what purpose these books serve.

Books are essentially paper—sheets of paper printed with letters and bound together. Their true purpose is to be read, to convey the information to their readers. It's the information they contain that has meaning. There is no meaning in their just being on your shelves. You read books for the experience of reading. Books you have read have already been experienced and their content is inside you, even if you don't remember. So when deciding which books to keep, forget about whether you think you'll read it again or whether you've mastered what's inside. Instead, take each book in your hand and decide whether it moves you or not. Keep only those books that will make you happy just to see them on your shelves, the ones that you really love. That includes this book, too. If you don't feel any joy when you hold it in your hand, I would rather you discard it.

What about books that you have started but not yet finished reading? Or books you bought but have not yet started? What should be done with books like these that you intend to read sometime? The Internet has made it easy to purchase books, but as a consequence, it seems to me that people have far more unread books than they once did, ranging from three to more than forty. It is not uncommon for people to purchase a book and then buy another one not long after, before they have read the first one. Unread books accumulate. The problem with books that we intend to read sometime is that they are far harder to part with than ones we have already read.

I remember one incident where I was giving a lesson to a CEO on how to clean his office. His bookshelves were filled with difficult-sounding titles that you might expect a company president to read, such as classics by authors like Drucker and Carnegie, as well as the latest best sellers. It was like walking into a bookstore. When I saw his collection, I had a sinking feeling. Sure enough, when he began sorting them, he put one book after another on his "to keep" pile, announcing that they were still unread. By the time he finished, he still had fifty volumes and had barely made a dent in the original collection. When I asked why he kept them, he gave the classic answer from my list of most probable answers: "Because I might want to read it sometime." I'm afraid that from personal experience I can tell you right now, "sometime" never comes.

If you missed your chance to read a particular book, even if it was recommended to you or is one you have been intending to read for ages, this is your chance to let it go. You may have wanted to read it when you bought it, but if you haven't read it by now, the book's purpose was to teach you that you didn't need it. There's no need to finish reading books that you only got halfway through. Their purpose was to be read halfway. So get rid of all those unread books. It will be far better for you to read the book that really grabs you right now than one that you left to gather dust for years.

People with large book collections are almost always diligent learners. This is why it's not unusual to see many references and study guides in my clients' bookcases. Those most commonly left unread in Japan are English textbooks, practical English conversation handbooks for travelers, and useful business English phrase books. Handbooks and guides for acquiring qualifications are often incredibly diverse, ranging from bookkeeping, real estate, and computer qualifications to aromatherapy and color coordinating. Sometimes I am amazed at the type of qualifications my clients are interested in. Many of my clients also keep their old textbooks all the way back to junior high and notebooks for practicing writing skills.

So if, like many of my clients, you have any books that fall into this category, I urge you to stop insisting that you will use them someday. Get rid of them today. Why? Because the odds are very low that you'll ever read them. Of all my clients, less than 15 percent put such books to use. When they explain why they hang on to them, their answers are all about what they intend to do "someday." "I'd like to study this someday," "I'll study it when I have a little more time," "I thought it would be useful to master English," "I wanted to study bookkeeping because I'm in management." If you haven't done what you intended to do yet, donate or recycle that book. Only by discarding it will you be able to test how passionate you are about that subject. If your feelings don't change after discarding it, then you're fine as is. If you want the book so badly after getting rid of it that you're willing to buy another copy, then buy one—and this time read and study it.

Books to keep

Those that belong in the hall of fame

I now keep my collection of books to about thirty volumes at any one time, but in the past, I found it very hard to discard books because I love them. The first time I sorted through my library using the yardstick of whether or not they gave me joy, I had about a hundred volumes left in my bookcase. Although this is not excessive compared to the average, I felt that I could still reduce. One day I decided to take a closer look at what I had. I started with books that I considered taboo to discard. In my case, first on the list was *Alice in Wonderland*, which I have read repeatedly since grade one. Books like this, which fall into one's personal Book Hall of Fame, are simple to identify. Next, I looked at books that inspired pleasure but didn't quite make it into the Hall of Fame. As time passes the content of this category naturally changes, but these books are the ones I definitely want to keep right now. At that time, one of these was *The Art of Discarding*, which first opened my eyes to tidying, although I no longer have it. Books that provide this degree of pleasure are also fine to keep.

The most difficult ones are those that give you moderate pleasure—those with words and phrases that moved your heart and that you might want to read again. These are the hardest to discard. Although I felt no pressure to get rid of them, I could not overlook the fact that they only gave me moderate pleasure, particularly not when I was pursuing perfection in the field of tidying. I began to search for a way to let them go without regret and eventually hit upon what I called the "bulk reduction method." Realizing that what I really wanted to keep was not the book but certain information or specific words it contained, I decided that if I kept only what was necessary, I should be able to part with the rest.

My idea was to copy the sentences that inspired me into a notebook. Over time, I thought, this would become a personal collection of my favorite words of wisdom. It might be fun to read it over in the future and trace the path my interests had led me. With great excitement, I pulled out a notebook I liked and launched my project. I began by underlining the places I wanted to copy. Then I wrote the title in my notebook and began transcribing. Once I started, however, I realized that this process was far too much work. It takes time to transcribe and if I was going to be able to read those words in the future, my handwriting had to be neat. To copy ten quotations from a single book would take at least half an hour, and that was a low estimate. The thought of doing this for forty books made me dizzy.

My next plan was to use a copy machine. I would copy the sections I wanted to keep and cut and paste them into the notebook. This, I thought, should be much quicker and easier. But when I tried it, it was even more work. I finally decided to rip the relevant page out of the book. Pasting pages into a notebook was also a pain, so I simplified the process by slipping them into a file instead. This only took five minutes per book and I managed to get rid of forty books and keep the words that I liked. I was extremely pleased with the results. Two years after launching this "bulk reduction method," I had a sudden flash of realization. I had never once looked at the file I created. All that effort had just been to ease my own conscience.

Recently, I have noticed that having fewer books actually increases the impact of the information I read. I recognize necessary information much more easily. Many of my clients, particularly those who have disposed of a substantial number of books and papers, have also mentioned this. For books, timing is everything. **The moment you first encounter a particular book is the right time to read it.** To avoid missing that moment, I recommend that you keep your collection small.

Sorting papers

Rule of thumb—discard everything

Once you've finished organizing your books, it's time to move on to your papers. For example, the letter holder bursting with envelopes that hangs on your wall; the school announcements stuck to your fridge; the unanswered invitation to your school reunion lying by the phone; the newspapers that have accumulated on your table over the last few days. There are several spots within the house where papers tend to pile up like snowdrifts.

Although the general assumption is that there are far fewer papers in the home than in an office, this is actually not true. The minimum amount of paper my clients discard or recycle is two 45-liter bags. The maximum (so far) is fifteen bags. I don't know how many times I hear my clients' paper shredders jam. It is extremely difficult to manage such a large volume of paper, yet I occasionally meet some amazing clients whose filing skills take my breath away. When I ask, "How are you managing your papers?" their explanations are extremely thorough.

"Papers related to the children go in this file. That file there is my recipe file. Magazine clippings go in here, and manuals for my electric appliances go in this box. . . ." They have categorized their papers in such fine detail that my mind sometimes wanders off in the middle of their discourse. I confess. I hate filing papers! I never use multiple files or write labels. This system perhaps works better in an office setting, where many people use the same documents, but there is absolutely no need to use such a detailed filing system in the home.

My basic principle for sorting papers is to throw them all away. My clients are stunned when I say this, but there is nothing more annoying than papers. After all, they will never inspire joy, no matter how carefully you keep them. For this reason, **I recommend you dispose of anything that does not fall into one of three categories: currently in use, needed for a limited period of time, or must be kept indefinitely.**

The term "papers," by the way, does not include papers with sentimental value like old love letters or diaries. Attempting to sort these will slow down your pace drastically. Limit yourself at first to sorting papers that give you no thrill at all and finish the job in one go. Letters from friends and lovers can be left for when you tackle sentimental items.

Once you've gone through those papers that don't evoke any pleasure, what should you do with the ones that you've decided to keep? My filing method is extremely simple. I divide them into two categories: papers to be saved and papers that need to be dealt with. Although my policy is to get rid of all papers, these are the only categories I make for those that can't be discarded. Letters requiring a reply, forms that need to be submitted, a newspaper that I intend to read—make a special corner for papers like these that need to be dealt with. **Make sure that you keep all such papers in one spot only. Never let them spread to other parts of the house.** I recommend using a vertical organizer in which papers can be stored standing up and designating a specific place for it. All papers requiring attention can be placed in here without separating them.

As for papers that must be saved, these I subdivide according to the frequency of use. Again, the way I divide them is not complicated. I organize them into infrequently used papers and more frequently used papers. Infrequently used papers include insurance policies, guarantees, and leases. Unfortunately, these must be kept automatically regardless of the fact that they spark no particular joy in your heart. As you will almost never need to access papers in this category, you don't have to put a lot of effort into storing them. I recommend putting them all into a single ordinary clear plastic folder without worrying about further categorization.

The other subcategory consists of papers that you will take out and look at more frequently, such as outlines of seminars or newspaper clippings. These are meaningless unless they are stored in a way that's easy to access and read, which is why I recommend inserting them into the book-like pages of a clear plastic file folder. This category is the trickiest of them all. Although papers like this are not really necessary, they tend to multiply. Reducing the volume of this category is key to organizing your papers.

Papers are organized into only three categories: needs attention, should be saved (contractual documents), and should be saved (others). The point is to keep all papers in one category in the same container or folder and to purposely refrain from subdividing them any further by content. In other words, you only need three containers or folders. Don't forget that the "needs attention" box ought to be empty. If there are papers in it, be aware that this means you have left things undone in your life that require your attention. Although I have never managed to completely empty my "needs attention" box, this is the goal to which we should aspire.

All about papers
How to organize troublesome papers

My basic policy is to discard all papers, but there are always going to be some that are hard to get rid of. Let's consider here how to tackle these.

LECTURE MATERIALS

Those who enjoy studying are quite likely to attend seminars or courses in various subjects, such as aromatherapy, logical thinking, or marketing. The recent trend in Japan is to utilize time in the early morning to take seminars. The content and time frame are broadening, giving people a wide choice. For the participants, the materials diligently produced by the lecturer are akin to a badge of honor, and as such they are hard to part with. But when I visit the homes of these ardent learners, I find that these materials usurp much of the room, making their space oppressive.

One of my clients was a woman in her thirties who worked for an advertising company. The moment I entered her room, I felt like I was in an office. My eyes were assaulted by rows of files with carefully printed titles. "These are all materials from the seminars I took," she told me. A self-confessed seminar fanatic, she had saved and filed the materials from every seminar she had ever attended.

People often insist, "I want to restudy these materials sometime," but most never do so. Moreover, the majority of them usually have materials for multiple seminars on the same or similar subjects. Why? Because what they learned at the seminars did not stick. I am not saying this as a criticism, but merely to point out why it isn't worth keeping materials from past seminars. If the content is not put into practice, such courses are meaningless. A seminar's value begins the moment we start attending, and the key to extracting the full value is putting what we learn there into practice the moment the course ends. Why do people pay expensive fees for such courses when they can read the same content in a book or elsewhere? Because they want to feel the passion of the teacher and experience that learning environment. Thus the real material is the seminar itself, and it must be experienced live.

When you attend a seminar, do so with the resolve to part with every handout distributed. If you regret recycling it, take the same seminar again, and this time apply the learning. **It's paradoxical, but I believe that precisely because we hang on to such materials, we fail to put what we learn into practice.** The biggest collection of seminar materials I have come across so far was 199 files. Needless to say, I had her discard every single one.

CREDIT CARD STATEMENTS

Another thing to discard are all your credit card statements. What is their purpose? For most people, they are simply the means of checking how much money was spent on what during a particular month. So, once you've checked the content to confirm that it's correct and have recorded the figure in your household account book, the statement has fulfilled its purpose and you should discard it. Trust me. You need feel no guilt at all.

Can you think of any other time that you would really need your credit card statements? Do you imagine that you might need them for a court case to prove how much was withdrawn? That's not going to happen, so there is no need to treasure these statements for the rest of your life. The same is true for notices of withdrawals from your account to pay utility fees. Be resolute and take this opportunity to get rid of them.

Of all my clients, the ones who had the hardest time disposing of papers were a couple, both of whom were lawyers. They kept asking, "What if this document is needed in court?" At first, they made very little progress, but in the end, even they were able to discard almost all their papers without experiencing any problems. If they can do it, so can you.

WARRANTIES FOR ELECTRICAL APPLIANCES

Whether a TV or a digital camera, all electrical appliances come with a warranty. This is the most standard document category in any home, and the one that almost everyone files and saves properly. The method of organizing, however, is usually almost but not quite right.

In general, people save their warranties in clear folder files or accordion-style files. The attraction of these files is that the documents can be stored in separate compartments. However, therein lies their pitfall. Because they are so well divided, it is easy to overlook things. Most people save not only the warranty but also the operation manual in the same file. First, let's start by parting with these manuals. Take a look at them. Have you ever used them? In general, there are only a few manuals that we actually need to read, such as our computer or digital camera manual, and these are so thick that they won't fit in a file anyway. So basically, any manuals contained in your warranty folder can be discarded without causing any difficulty.

To date, all my clients have discarded most of their manuals, including those for their PCs and cameras, and none of them has experienced any problems from doing so. If they have a problem, they can usually fix it themselves by fiddling with the machine, and they can find solutions for anything they can't figure out on their own from the Internet or the place of purchase. So I assure you, you can dispose of them without any qualms.

Getting back to warranties: the filing method I recommend is to put them all in a single clear file, without separating them into categories. Warranties are only used once a year if at all. What point is there in carefully sorting and separating them when the odds that they will be needed are so low? Moreover, if you've filed them in a file folder, you'll have to flip through the pages to find the right warranty. In that case, it's just as easy to keep them all in one file, pull out the entire stack, and search through it.

If you sort in too much detail, it means you will have fewer opportunities to look at each warranty. Before you realize it, the warranty will be out of date. If you have to sift through them all when you need one anyway, this becomes an excellent opportunity to check the expiration dates of your other warranties. This way, you don't have to go to the trouble of deliberately checking the contents just for the expiration dates, and often, you don't even have to buy the clear file in which you store the warranties because there is usually at least one already in the house. Finally, this method takes up a tenth of the space of conventional methods.

GREETING CARDS

In Japan, it is the custom to send New Year's cards to convey New Year's greetings (many have lottery numbers at the bottom). This means that each card has fulfilled its purpose the moment the receiver finishes reading it. Once you've checked to see whether the numbers on your cards have won anything in the lottery, you can part with the cards with gratitude for conveying to you the consideration of the sender. If you save the cards to confirm the sending address for the following year, then only save one year's worth. Dispense with those that are two or more years old, except those that spark joy in your heart.

USED CHECKBOOKS

Used checkbooks are just that—used. You're not going to look at them again, and even if you do, it won't increase the amount of money in the bank, so, really, get rid of them.

PAY SLIPS

The purpose of your pay slip is to inform you how much you have been paid for this month. Once you've checked the content, its usefulness is over.

Komono (miscellaneous items)

Keep things because you love them—
not "just because"

I pull out a drawer in a client's home and discover a
strange little box, just waiting to be opened—like a
tantalizing book that promises some fascinating tale. But
for me there is no excitement whatsoever. I know exactly
what I'll find inside. Loose change, hairpins, erasers, spare
buttons, wristwatch parts, batteries that may or may not
be dead, leftover medicine, lucky charms, key rings. And
the list goes on. I already know what the client's answer
will be if I ask why these things are in that box: "Just
because."

Many items within the home are treated in the
same way. They are placed, stored, and accumulate "just
because," without our giving them much thought. I call
this category *komono*, a Japanese term that the dictionary
defines variously as "small articles; miscellaneous items;
accessories; gadgets or small tools, parts, or attachments;
an insignificant person; small fry." It's no wonder people
don't know what to do with things that fall into such a
vague and all-encompassing category. Still, it's time to
bid farewell to this "just because" approach. These items
play an important part in supporting your lifestyle and
therefore they, too, deserve to be handled one by one and
sorted properly.

Unlike clothes or books, this category includes a diverse range of items, and the thought of trying to sort and organize them may seem daunting. If you deal with them in the proper order, however, this task is actually quite simple. The basic order for sorting *komono* is as follows:

1. CDs, DVDs

2. Skin care products

3. Makeup

4. Accessories

5. Valuables (passports, credit cards, etc.)

6. Electrical equipment and appliances (digital cameras, electric cords, anything that seems vaguely "electric")

7. Household equipment (stationery and writing materials, sewing kits, etc.)

8. Household supplies (expendables like medicine, detergents, tissues, etc.)

9. Kitchen goods/food supplies (spatulas, pots, blenders, etc.)

10. Other (spare change, figurines, etc.)

(If you have many items related to a particular interest or hobby, such as ski equipment or tea ceremony articles, treat these as a single subcategory.)

I recommend this particular order because it is easier if you start with more personal items and clearly defined content first. If you live alone, you don't really need to worry about the order as long as you do one subcategory at a time. **Too many people live surrounded by things they don't need "just because."** I urge you to take stock of your *komono* and save only, and I mean only, those that bring you joy.

Common types of *komono*

Disposables

A surprising number of things are instantly identifiable as disposable without even asking, "Does this spark joy?" I have already pointed out how important it is to relinquish the things that you find it hard to part with. It is equally important when putting your house in order to actually notice the things you have kept for "no particular reason." The majority of people are surprisingly unaware of the odds and ends taking up space in their homes.

GIFTS

A plate received as a wedding favor that still sits in its box on top of the china cabinet. A key holder you received as a souvenir from a friend that now lies in your drawer.

A set of peculiar-smelling incense presented to you by your colleagues on your birthday. What do these items all have in common? They were gifts. Someone important to you used precious time to pick them out and buy them for you. They are an expression of love and consideration. You can't just throw them away, right?

But let's consider this more carefully. Most of these gifts remain unopened or have been used only once. Admit it. They simply don't suit your taste. The true purpose of a present is *to be received*. **Presents are not "things" but a means for conveying someone's feelings.** When viewed from this perspective, you don't need to feel guilty for parting with a gift. Just thank it for the joy it gave you when you first received it. Of course, it would be ideal if you could use it with joy. But surely the person who gave it to you doesn't want you to use it out of a sense of obligation, or to put it away without using it, only to feel guilty every time you see it. When you discard or donate it, you do so for the sake of the giver, too.

COSMETIC SAMPLES SAVED FOR TRIPS

Do you have a collection of cosmetic samples that have been hanging around for a year or more unused? Many people keep these to use on trips, but then never seem to take them when they travel. I contacted various manufacturers to inquire about the shelf life of these products. The answers were varied. Some only last a few weeks, while others are good for a year. When the quantity is very small, such as for samples, the quality deteriorates faster. To use possibly outdated cosmetics, especially when you are supposed to be enjoying your travels, seems rather foolhardy.

ELECTRONICS PACKAGES

Boxes are surprisingly bulky. Discard or recycle the box your cell phone comes in as soon as you unpack it. You don't need the manual or the CD that comes with it either. You'll figure out the applications you need through using it. All of my clients have discarded these things yet none of them has ever been inconvenienced by their absence. If you do have a problem, you can always get help from the Internet or the clerk at the shop where you bought it. It is far quicker to ask a pro for the answer than to struggle to find one in the manual by yourself.

Some people save the boxes for electrical appliances because they think they can get more money for the appliances if they ever sell them. This, however, is a waste. If you consider the rent or mortgage you pay, turning your space into a storage shed for empty boxes costs you more than what you could earn selling an appliance in a box. You don't need to keep them for moving either. You can worry about finding suitable boxes when the time comes. It's a shame to let a boring box take up room in your house just because you might need it someday.

UNIDENTIFIED CORDS

If you see a cord and wonder what on earth it's for, chances are you'll never use it again. **Mysterious cords will always remain just that—a mystery.** Are you worried you might need it if something breaks? Don't be. I have seen count-less homes with duplicates of the same type of cord, but a tangle of cords just makes it harder to find the right one. In the end, it is quicker to buy a new one. Keep only those cords that you can clearly identify and get rid of the rest. Your collection most likely contains quite a few that belong to defunct machines you have long since discarded.

BROKEN APPLIANCES

I often come across broken TVs and radios in my clients' homes. Obviously, there is no need to keep these. If you, too, have broken appliances, see this as an opportunity to contact your local recycler and get rid of them.

BEDDING FOR THE GUEST WHO NEVER COMES

Quilts, pillows, blankets, sheets—spare sets of bedding take up a lot of room. This is another common item that gets discarded during my lessons, and again, my clients rarely miss it. Although it's worth having spare bedding if you have regular guests, it's unnecessary to keep extra sets if you only have overnight visitors at most once or twice a year. Bedding stored indefinitely in the closet often smells so mildewed you wouldn't want to let your guests use it anyway. Take a whiff and see for yourself.

SPARE BUTTONS

You will never use spare buttons. In most cases, when a button falls off, it's a sign that the particular shirt or blouse has been well worn and loved and has now reached the end of its life. For coats and jackets that you want to keep for a long time, I recommend sewing spare buttons to the lining when you first buy them. For other clothes, if you lose a button and really want to replace it, you can always get what you need at a large handicrafts shop. From my work in the field, I have come to the conclusion that when a button falls off, people often don't bother to sew another one on even when they have kept the spares. Instead, they either keep wearing the outfit without a button or leave it lying around somewhere in their wardrobe. If you're not going to use spare buttons anyway, it shouldn't matter that you get rid of them.

PRODUCTS FROM THE LATEST HEALTH CRAZE

Slimming belts, glass bottles for making kefir, a special blender for making tofu, a weight-loss machine that mimics the movement of horseback riding—it seems a waste to get rid of expensive items like these that you bought by mail order but never fully used. Believe me,

I can relate. But you can let them go. The exhilaration you felt when you bought them is what counts. Express your appreciation for their contribution to your life by telling them, "Thank you for the boost you gave me when I bought you," or "Thank you for helping me get a little more fit." Then discard them with the conviction that you are healthier for having bought them.

FREE NOVELTY GOODS

A cell phone screen cleaner that came with a soda bottle, a ball pen engraved with your school's name, a paper fan you got at an event, a set of plastic cups won at a fair, glasses bearing a beer company's logo, Post-its stamped with a pharmaceutical company's name, a folder with just five sheets of blotting paper, a promotional calendar (still in its tube), a pocket calendar (unused even six months into the year). None of these are going to bring you any pleasure. Discard or recycle them without any qualms.

Small change

Make "into my wallet" your motto

Do you have loose change lying around—a penny or two in the bottom of your purse, a dime in the back of a drawer, a quarter on the table? I always find coins when I'm helping clients put their house in order. The king of the *komono* category, coins can be found in the entrance hall, the kitchen, the living room, the washroom, on top of furniture, and inside drawers. **Despite the fact that coins are perfectly good cash, they are treated with far less respect than paper money.** It seems strange that they should be left lying around the house where they are of no use at all.

Whenever my clients come across loose change during tidying, I make sure it goes straight into their wallets—never into a piggybank. Unlike the other categories, you don't need to gather coins from every part of the house. Instead, just pop them into your wallet whenever you stumble on them. If you put them in a piggybank, you are simply transferring the place where they will be ignored. People who have lived in the same house for a long time are particularly prone to forgetting about their little cache of coins. Frankly, no one I've met who saved pennies without a clear purpose has ever actually used them. If you are saving coins with the vague idea that it would be nice to see how many you can accumulate, now is the time to take them to the bank. The longer you wait, the heavier your cache will be, and the more bother to take it to the bank.

I have also noticed that for some unfathomable reason many of my clients start saving coins in bags when their piggybank is full. Years later during my course, they stumble across a bag bursting with coins in the back of a cupboard. By that time, it is pungent with the smell of rust and mold, the coins are discolored, and they make a dull clinking sound instead of jingling. At this point, my clients would rather just ignore the bag's existence. Writing this description is hard enough, but to actually see these coins, stripped of their dignity as money, is heartrending. I beg you to rescue those forgotten coins wasting away in your home by adopting the motto "into my wallet!"

Sentimental items

Your parents' home is not a haven for mementos

Now that you have organized your clothes, books, papers, and *komono*, you can finally tackle the last category—items that have sentimental value. I leave this for last because these are the hardest things to discard. Just as the word implies, mementos are reminders of a time when these items gave us joy. The thought of disposing of them sparks the fear that we'll lose those precious memories along with them. But you don't need to worry. Truly precious memories will never vanish even if you discard the objects associated with them. When you think about your future, is it worth keeping mementos of things that you would otherwise forget? We live in the present. **No matter how wonderful things used to be, we cannot live in the past. The joy and excitement we feel here and now are more important.** So, once again, the way to decide what to keep is to pick up each item and ask yourself, "Does this spark joy?"

Let me tell you about a client of mine whom I'll call "A." She was a thirty-year-old mother of two in a five-member household. When I visited her house for our second session, it was obvious that the number of things in her home had decreased. "You really worked hard," I said. "It looks like you must have gotten rid of about thirty bags' worth of stuff."

Looking very pleased, she said, "Yes, I did! I sent all my keepsakes to my mother's place." I could hardly believe my ears. She had used the "send it to my parents" method of tidying. When I first started this business, I actually thought that being able to send things "home" was the privilege of people who came from large houses in the country. The majority of my clients were single women or young mothers living in Tokyo. If they asked permission to send things to their parents' house, I said, "Sure. As long as you do it right away." I never thought anything of this until my clientele expanded to homes in rural towns. When I learned the true state of parents' houses, I was forced to retract my rash words.

Now I realize that people who have a convenient place to send things, such as a parents' house, are actually quite unfortunate. Even if the house is large with rooms to spare, it is not some infinitely expanding fourth dimension. **People never retrieve the boxes they send "home." Once sent, they will never again be opened.**

But let me get back to my story. Sometime later, A's mother started taking my course. I knew that if she were to graduate, we would have to do something about the luggage A had sent home. When I visited the house, I found that A's room had been left untouched. Her things filled the bookcase and the closet, and now there were two big boxes parked on the floor. Her mother's dream was to have a space of her own in which she could relax, but even though A had moved out long ago, with her things still enshrined in her room, the only space her mother felt was hers was the kitchen. This seemed very unnatural. I contacted A and announced, "You and your mother won't graduate from this course until you have both dealt with the stuff you left at your parents' house."

On the day of her last lesson, A looked extremely happy. "Now I can enjoy the rest of my life free from care!" She had gone back home and put her things in order. In the boxes, she had found a diary, photographs of old boyfriends, a mountain of letters and New Year's cards, and more. "I was just fooling myself by sending the things I couldn't bear to part with to my parents. When I looked at each item again, I realized that I had lived those moments to the fullest and I was able to thank my keepsakes for the joy they gave me at the time. When I threw them away, I felt like I was confronting my past for the first time in my life."

That's right. **By handling each sentimental item and deciding what to discard, you process your past.** If you just stow these things away in a drawer or cardboard box, before you realize it, your past will become a weight that holds you back and keeps you from living in the here and now. To put your things in order means to put your past in order, too. It's like resetting your life and settling your accounts so that you can take the next step forward.

Another item that is just as difficult to discard is keepsakes from one's children. A Father's Day present with the words "Thanks, Dad." A picture your son drew that was selected by the teacher to hang in the school hall, or an ashtray your daughter made. If these things still bring you joy, it is fine to keep them. But if your children are already grown and you are keeping them because you think discarding them will hurt your children's feelings, ask them. They are quite likely to say, "What? You still have that? Go ahead and get rid of it."

And what about things from your own childhood? Do you still keep your report cards or graduation certificates? When my client pulled out a school uniform from forty years ago, even I felt my heart constrict with emotion. But it still should be disposed of. Let all those letters you received years ago from a girlfriend or boyfriend go. The purpose of a letter is fulfilled the moment it is received. By now, the person who wrote it has long forgotten what he or she wrote and even the letter's very existence. As for accessories you received as gifts, keep them only if they bring you pure joy. If you are keeping them because you can't forget a former boyfriend, it's better to discard or donate them. Hanging on to them makes it more likely that you will miss opportunities for new relationships.

It is not our memories but the person we have become because of those past experiences that we should treasure. This is the lesson these keepsakes teach us when we sort them. The space in which we live should be for the person we are becoming now, not for the person we were in the past.

Photos

Cherish who you are now

If you have been sorting and discarding things in the order I recommend, you have likely stumbled across photographs in many different places, perhaps stuck between books on a shelf, lying in a desk drawer, or hidden in a box of odds and ends. While many may already have been in albums, I'm sure you found the odd photo or two enclosed with a letter or still encased in the envelope from the photo shop. (I don't know why so many people leave photos in these envelopes.) Because photos tend to emerge from the most unexpected places when we are sorting other categories, it is much more efficient to put them in a designated spot every time you find one and deal with them all at the very end.

There is a good reason to leave photos for last. If you start sorting photos before you have honed your intuitive sense of what brings you joy, the whole process will spin out of control and come to a halt. In contrast, once you have followed the correct order for tidying (i.e., clothes, books, papers, *komono*, sentimental items), sorting will proceed smoothly, and you will be amazed by your capacity to choose on the basis of what gives you pleasure.

There is only one way to sort photos, and you should keep in mind that it takes a little time. The correct method is to remove all your photos from their albums and look at them one by one. Those who protest that this is far too much work are people who have never truly sorted photos. Photographs exist only to show a specific event or time. For this reason, they must be looked at one by one. When you do this, you will be surprised at how clearly you can tell the difference between those that touch your heart and those that don't. As always, only keep the ones that inspire joy.

With this method, you will keep only about five per day of a special trip, but this will be so representative of that time that they bring back the rest vividly. Really important things are not that great in number. Unexciting photos of scenery that you can't even place belong in the garbage. The meaning of a photo lies in the excitement and joy you feel when taking it. In many cases, the prints developed afterward have already outlived their purpose.

Sometimes people keep a mass of photos in a big box with the intention of enjoying them someday in their old age. I can tell you now that "someday" never comes. I can't count how many boxes of unsorted photographs I have seen that were left by someone who has passed away. A typical conversation with my clients goes something like this:

"What's in that box?"

"Photos."

"Then you can leave them to sort at the end."

"Oh, but they aren't mine. They belonged to my grandfather."

Every time I have this conversation it makes me sad. I can't help thinking that the lives of the deceased would have been that much richer if the space occupied by that box had been free when the person was alive. Besides, we shouldn't still be sorting photos when we reach old age. If you, too, are leaving this task for when you grow old, don't wait. Do it now. You will enjoy the photos far more when you are old if they are already in an album than if you have to move and sort through a heavy boxful of them.

Astounding stockpiles I have seen

There are two surprises I frequently encounter when helping clients put their houses in order: highly unusual items and sheer numbers. I come across the first every time. It might be a music machine used by a singer or the latest cooking utensils owned by someone who loves to cook. Every day provides exciting encounters with the unknown. This is only natural, as my clients' interests and professions are extremely diverse.

The real shock is when I discover a massive stockpile of a simple item that you would find in any home. As we work, I always jot down the rough volume of different items my clients own and particularly keep an eye on my stockpile ranking for different items because new records are constantly being made. Once, for example, I discovered a huge stock of toothbrushes in a client's home. The record up to that point had been thirty-five. Even that collection seemed large. "Perhaps you have a few more than you need," I remarked and we enjoyed a little laugh together. But the new record far surpassed the old. This client had sixty toothbrushes! Arranged in boxes in the cupboard under the sink, they looked like a work of art. It's interesting how the human mind tries to make sense even out of the nonsensical. I found myself pondering whether she would go through one a day if she brushed her teeth too hard, or if perhaps she used a different brush for each tooth.

Another surprise was a stock of thirty boxes of plastic kitchen wrap. I opened the cupboard above the kitchen sink to find it completely filled with an array of what looked like large yellow LEGO blocks. "I use plastic wrap every day so it goes down fast," my client explained. But even if she used one box a week that supply would last her over half a year. Regular-size wrap comes in twenty-meter rolls. To use up one roll a week, you would have to cover an eight-inch-diameter plate sixty-six times, even allowing for rather generous use. Just the thought of repeating the action of pulling and tearing plastic wrap that many times would give me carpal tunnel syndrome.

As for toilet paper, the record stock so far is eighty rolls. "I have loose bowels you see . . . I run out very quickly," was the client's excuse. But even if she used one roll a day, she had at least a three months' supply. I'm not sure she could have used up one roll a day even if she spent all day wiping her bottom, and by that time her bottom would have been rubbed raw. It made me wonder whether I should be giving her skin cream rather than lessons in cleaning.

The ultimate record, however, was a stockpile of 20,000 cotton swabs, a cache of one hundred boxes with two hundred swabs each. If my client used one swab a day, it would take her fifty-five years to use up her supply. By the time she had finished, she might have developed amazing techniques for cleaning her ears. The last swab used on the last day would appear almost sacred.

You may find these accounts hard to believe, but I'm not kidding. The strange thing is that these clients never realized how many items they actually had until they began putting their house in order. And even though they owned a huge stockpile, they always felt as if they didn't have enough and were anxious about running out. For people who stockpile, I don't think there is any amount that would make them feel secure. The more they have, the more they worry about running out and the more anxious they become. Even though they still have two left, they will go out and buy five more.

Unlike a shop, if you run out of something at home, it's not a big deal. It may cause you temporary stress, but it does no irreparable damage. But how should we handle these stockpiles? Although the best solution would appear to be to use all the items up, in many cases they are past their expiration date and must be thrown out. I highly recommend that you get rid of excess stock all at once. Give it away to friends who need it, recycle it, or take it to a donation shop. You may think this is a waste of money, but reducing your stock and relieving yourself of the burden of excess is the quickest and most effective way to put your things in order.

Once you've experienced the freedom of a life without surplus stock, you won't want to give it up and will naturally stop stockpiling. My clients tell me that now life is more fun because when they run out of something they enjoy seeing how long they can last without it or trying to substitute other things. It's important to assess what you have on hand now and eliminate excess.

Reduce until you reach the point where something clicks

Sort by category, in the correct order, and keep only those things that inspire joy. Do this thoroughly and quickly, all in one go. If you follow this advice, you will dramatically reduce the volume of things you own, experience an exhilaration you have never known before, and gain confidence in your life.

What is the perfect amount of possessions? I think that most people don't know. If you have lived in Japan or the United States all your life, you have almost certainly been surrounded by far more than you need. This makes it hard for many people to imagine how much they need to live comfortably. **As you reduce your belongings through the process of tidying, you will come to a point where you suddenly know how much is just right for you.** You will feel it as clearly as if something has clicked inside your head and said, "Ah! This is just the amount I need to live comfortably. This is all I need to be happy. I don't need anything more." The satisfaction that envelops your whole being at that point is palpable. I call this the "just-right click point." Interestingly, once you have passed this point, you'll find that the amount you own never increases. And that is precisely why you will never rebound.

The click point differs from one person to another. For a shoe lover, it might be one hundred pairs of shoes, while a book lover might not need anything but books. Some people, like me, have more loungewear than clothes for going out, while others may prefer to go naked in the home and therefore have no loungewear at all. (You'd be surprised at how many fall into this latter category.)

As you put your house in order and decrease your possessions, you'll see what your true values are, what is really important to you in your life. But don't focus on reducing, or on efficient storage methods, for that matter. Focus instead on choosing the things that inspire joy and on enjoying life according to your own standards. This is the true pleasure of tidying. If you have not yet felt a click, don't worry. You can still reduce. Tackle this job with confidence.

Follow your intuition and all will be well

"Choose those things that spark joy when you touch them."

"Hang those clothes that would be happier on hangers."

"Don't worry about throwing away too much. There will come a moment when you know what is just right."

If you have read this far, you have probably noticed that in my method your feelings are the standard for decision making. Many people may be puzzled by such vague criteria as "things that give you a thrill of pleasure" or "click point." The majority of methods give clearly defined numerical goals, such as "Discard anything you haven't used for two years," "Seven jackets and ten blouses is the perfect amount," "Get rid of one thing every time you buy something new." But I believe this is one reason these methods result in rebound.

Even if these methods temporarily result in a tidy space, automatically following criteria proposed by others and based on their "know-how" will have no lasting effect—unless their criteria happens to match your own standards of what feels right. Only you can know what kind of environment makes you feel happy. The act of picking up and choosing objects is extremely personal. To avoid rebound, you need to create your own tidying method with your own standards. This is precisely why it is so important to identify how you feel about each item you own.

The fact that you possess a surplus of things that you can't bring yourself to discard doesn't mean you are taking good care of them. In fact, it is quite the opposite. By paring down to the volume that you can properly handle, you revitalize your relationship with your belongings. Just because you dispose of something does not mean you give up past experiences or your identity. Through the process of selecting only those things that inspire joy, you can identify precisely what you love and what you need.

When we honestly confront the things we own, they evoke many emotions within us. Those feelings are real. It is these emotions that give us the energy for living. **Believe what your heart tells you when you ask, "Does this spark joy?"** If you act on that intuition, you will be amazed at how things will begin to connect in your life and at the dramatic changes that follow. It is as if your life has been touched by magic. Putting your house in order is the magic that creates a vibrant and happy life.

4
—

Storing your things
to make your life shine

Designate a place for each thing

This is the routine I follow every day when I return from work. First, I unlock the door and announce to my house, "I'm home!" Picking up the pair of shoes I wore yesterday and left out in the entranceway, I say, "Thank you very much for your hard work," and put them away in the shoe cupboard. Then I take off the shoes I wore today and place them neatly in the entranceway. Heading to the kitchen, I put the kettle on and go to my bedroom. There I lay my handbag gently on the soft sheepskin rug and take off my outdoor clothes. I put my jacket and dress on a hanger, say, "Good job!" and hang them temporarily from the closet doorknob. I put my tights in a laundry basket that fits into the bottom right corner of my closet, open a drawer, select the clothes I feel like wearing inside, and get dressed. I greet the waist-high potted plant by the window and stroke its leaves.

My next task is to empty the contents of my handbag on the rug and put each item away in its place. First I remove all the receipts. Then I put my wallet in its designated box in a drawer under my bed with a word of gratitude. I place my train pass and my business card holder beside it. I put my wristwatch in a pink antique case in the same drawer and place my necklace and earrings on the accessory tray beside it. Before closing the drawer, I say, "Thanks for all you did for me today."

Next, I return to the entrance and put away the books and notebooks I carried around all day (I have converted a shelf of my shoe cupboard into a bookshelf). From the shelf below it I take out my "receipt pouch" and put my receipts in it. Then I put my digital camera that I use for work in the space beside it, which is reserved for electrical things. Papers that I've finished with go in the recycle bin beneath the kitchen range. In the kitchen, I make a pot of tea while checking the mail, disposing of the letters I've finished with.

I return to my bedroom, put my empty handbag in a bag, and put it on the top shelf of the closet, saying, "You did well. Have a good rest." From the time I get in the door to the moment I close the closet, a total of only five minutes has passed. Now I can go back to the kitchen, pour myself a cup of tea, and relax.

I did not give you this account to boast about my beautiful lifestyle, but rather to demonstrate what it's like to have a designated spot for everything. Keeping your space tidy becomes second nature. You can do it effortlessly, even when you come home tired from work, and this gives you more time to really enjoy life.

The point in deciding specific places to keep things is to designate a spot for *every* thing. You may think, "It would take me forever to do that," but you don't need to worry. Although it seems like deciding on a place for every item must be complicated, it's far simpler than deciding what to keep and what to discard. Since you have already decided what to keep according to type of item and since those items all belong to the same category, all you need to do is store them near each other.

The reason every item must have a designated place is because the existence of an item without a home multiplies the chances that your space will become cluttered again. Let's say, for example, that you have a shelf with nothing on it. What happens if someone leaves an object that has no designated spot on that shelf? That one item will become your downfall. Within no time that space, which had maintained a sense of order, will be covered with objects, as if someone had yelled, "Gather round, everybody!"

You only need to designate a spot for every item once. Try it. You'll be amazed at the results. No longer will you buy more than you need. No longer will the things you own continue to accumulate. In fact, your stock on hand will decrease. The essence of effective storage is this: designate a spot for every last thing you own. If you ignore this basic principle and start experimenting with the vast range of storage ideas being promoted, you will be sorry. Those storage "solutions" are really just prisons within which to bury possessions that spark no joy.

One of the main reasons for rebound is the failure to designate a spot for each item. Without a designated spot, where are you going to put things when you finish using them? Once you choose a place for your things, you can keep your house in order. So decide where your things belong and when you finish using them, put them there. This is the main requirement for storage.

Discard first, store later

The participants of my courses are all very surprised when I show them the before-and-after pictures of my clients' places. The most common response is "The room looks so bare!" It's true. In many cases, my clients choose to leave nothing on the floor and nothing to obstruct the line of vision. Even the bookcases have disappeared. But this doesn't mean they have cast off all their books. Rather, the bookcases are now in the closet or cupboard. Putting bookcases in the cupboard is one of my standard storage practices. If your closet is already filled to bursting, you may think that your bookcase would never fit. In fact, 99 percent of my readers probably feel this way. But there is actually plenty of room.

The amount of storage space you have in your room is actually just right. I can't count how many times people have complained to me that they don't have enough room, but I have yet to see a house that lacked sufficient storage. The real problem is that we have far more than we need or want. **Once you learn to choose your belongings properly, you will be left only with the amount that fits perfectly in the space you currently own.** This is the true magic of tidying. It may seem incredible, but my method of keeping only what sparks joy in the heart is really that precise. This is why you must begin by discarding. Once you have done that, it's easy to decide where things should go because your possessions will have been reduced to a third or even a quarter of what you started out with. Conversely, no matter how hard you tidy and no matter how effective the storage method, if you start storing before you have eliminated excess, you will rebound. I know because I've been there myself.

Yes, me. Even though I am warning you not to become a storage expert, even though I urge you to forget about storing until you have reduced your possessions, not long ago, 90 percent of my thoughts were focused solely on storage. I began thinking seriously about this issue from the time I was five, so this part of my career lasted even longer than my passion for discarding, which I only discovered as a teenager. During that period, I spent most of my time with a book or magazine in one hand trying out every kind of storage method and making every possible mistake.

Whether it was my own room, my siblings' rooms, or even my school, I spent my days examining what was in the drawers and cupboards and moving things a few millimeters at a time, trying to find the perfect arrangement. "What would happen if I moved this box over there?" "What would happen if I took out this divider?" No matter where I was, I would close my eyes and rearrange the contents of a cupboard or room in my mind as if they were pieces of a jigsaw puzzle. Having spent my youth steeped in this topic, I fell under the illusion that storage was some form of intellectual contest, the object of which was to see how much I could fit into a storage space by rational organization. If there were a gap between two pieces of furniture, I would squeeze in a storage unit and stack it with things, gloating triumphantly when the space was filled. Somewhere along the way, I had begun to see my things and even my house as an adversary that I had to beat, and I was constantly in fighting mode.

Storage: pursue ultimate simplicity

When I first started this business, I assumed that I had to demonstrate my ability to come up with miraculous storage designs—clever solutions that you might see in a magazine, such as a set of shelves that fit perfectly into a tiny space that no one else would have thought to use. I had some strange notion that this was the only way to satisfy my clients. In the end, however, such clever ideas are almost always impractical to use and serve only to gratify the designer's ego.

Just to give an example, once when I was helping to organize a client's home, I came across a turntable, much like those used underneath revolving tabletops in Chinese restaurants. It had originally served as the base of a microwave, but the oven was long gone. As soon as I saw it,

I had the brilliant idea of turning it into a storage item. I was having trouble deciding where it could be used as it was quite large and thick, but then my client happened to mention that she had so many salad dressings she could not keep them organized. I opened the cupboard she indicated and, sure enough, it was filled with bottles of salad dressing. I took them all out and tried inserting the turntable. It fit perfectly. I loaded it up and voilà! I had a storage space that looked as neat and fancy as a store display. She could get at the bottles in the back simply by turning the table. How convenient! My client was thrilled and everything seemed perfect.

It was not long before I realized my mistake. At our next lesson, I checked her kitchen. While most of it was still neat and tidy, when I opened the door of the cupboard under the sink, I saw that the inside was a mess. When I asked why, she explained that every time she spun the turntable, the bottles slid and fell over. In addition, she had too many bottles, so she rested the extra on the edge of the turntable, making it harder to spin.

As you can see, I had been so focused on using the turntable to create an amazing storage space that I had failed to really see what I was storing—bottles that slide and topple easily. When I thought about it more carefully, I also realized that no one needs frequent access to stock at the back of a cupboard, so there was no need for a turntable. Besides, round shapes take up too much room and create wasted space, which makes them unsuitable for storage. In the end, I removed the turntable, placed the bottles in a square box and returned them to the cupboard. Although plain and conventional, according to my client this method was far easier to use. From this experience, I came to the conclusion that storage methods should be as simple as possible. There is no point in thinking up complicated strategies. When in doubt, ask your house and the item being stored what is the best solution.

Most people realize that clutter is caused by too much stuff. But why do we have too much stuff? Usually it is because we do not accurately grasp how much we actually own. And we fail to grasp how much we own because our storage methods are too complex. The ability to avoid excess stock depends on the ability to simplify storage. The secret to maintaining an uncluttered room is to **pursue ultimate simplicity in storage** so that you can tell at a glance how much you have. I say "ultimate simplicity" for a reason. It is impossible to remember the existence of every item we own even when we simplify our storage methods. There are still times in my own house, where I have worked hard to keep storage simple, that I notice an item I had completely forgotten about in a closet or drawer. If my storage were more complex—for example, if I divided my things into three levels according to frequency of use or according to season—I am sure that many more items would be left to rot in the darkness. Therefore, it makes more sense to keep storage as simple as possible.

Don't scatter storage spaces

For the reasons described above, my storage method is extremely simple. **I have only two rules: store all items of the same type in the same place and don't scatter storage space.**

There are only two ways of categorizing belongings: by type of item and by person. This is easy to grasp if you consider someone who lives alone as opposed to someone who lives with family. If you live alone or have a room of your own, storage is very simple—just designate one place for storing each type of item. You can keep categories to a minimum by following those used for sorting. Start with clothes, then books, then documents, *komono*, and finally mementos. If you are sorting your things in this order, you can store each category in its own designated spot as soon as you have chosen what to keep.

You can even categorize more loosely than that. Instead of dividing your things by detailed type, use broad similarities in material, such as "cloth-like," "paper-like," and "things that are electrical," as your criteria and choose one place for each of these. This is much easier than trying to visualize where you might use an object or the frequency with which you use it. With my method, you will be able to categorize your things more accurately.

If you have already been selecting what to keep on the basis of what speaks to your heart, then you will understand what I mean because you have already collected items by category, spread them out in one spot, and held them in your hand to make your decision. The work you have been doing has actually honed your ability to sense what belongs together and to choose appropriate places for storing them.

If you live with your family, first clearly define separate storage spaces for each family member. This is essential. For example, you can designate separate closets for you, your husband, and your children, and store whatever belongs to each person in his or her respective closet. That's all you need to do. The important point here is to designate only one place per person if at all possible. In other words, storage should be focused in one spot. If storage places are spread around, the entire house will become cluttered in no time. To concentrate the belongings of each person in one spot is the most effective way for keeping storage tidy.

I once had a client who asked me to help her child be tidy. Her daughter was three years old. When I visited her house, I found that her daughter's things were stored in three different places: clothes in the bedroom, toys in the living room, and books in the Japanese tatami room. Following the basic principles of sorting and storing, we gathered everything in the tatami room. From that time on, her daughter began to choose her own clothes to wear and put away her things where they belonged. Although I was the one who had given the instructions, I was surprised. Even a three-year-old can tidy!

Having your own space makes you happy. Once you feel that it belongs to you personally, you want to keep it tidy. If it is hard to give everyone his or her own room, you can still give each person his or her own storage space. Of the many people I've met who are not good at tidying, most had parents who cleaned their rooms for them or they never had a space that they felt was their very own. These people often store their clothes in their children's dresser and their books in their partner's bookcase. But not having a space you can call your own is dangerous. **Everyone needs a sanctuary.**

I realize that when you begin tidying, there is a real temptation to start with spaces or things that belong to the entire household, such as the living room, soaps and medicines, or various appliances and household supplies. But please leave those for later. First, start by sorting only your own things. Choose what you want to keep and store it in your very own space. By doing so, you will learn the basics of how to put your house in order. Just as with choosing which belongings to keep, following the right order is crucial.

Forget about "flow planning" and "frequency of use"

Serious books on tidying commonly advise their readers to consider the flow plan when designing storage. I am not saying this advice is erroneous. There are many people who advocate practical storage methods based on careful consideration of the line of traffic in the house, so what I am saying here is intended to apply only to my own storage method. And I say, forget about flow planning.

When one of my clients, a woman in her fifties, had finished sorting and storing her own things, we tackled her husband's belongings. She told me that her husband had to have everything right at hand, whether it was the remote control or a book. When I examined their living space, I found that, indeed, her husband's things were stored all over the house. There was a small bookshelf for his books beside the toilet, a place for his bags in the entrance hall, and drawers for his socks and underwear near the bath. But that did not affect my policy. I always insist that storage be focused in a single place and therefore I told my client to move her husband's underwear, socks, and bags into the closet where his suits were hanging. She looked a bit anxious. "But he likes to keep things where he uses them," she said. "What if he's upset. . . ."

A common mistake many people make is to decide where to store things on the basis of where it's easiest to take them out. This approach is a fatal trap. **Clutter is caused by a failure to return things to where they belong. Therefore, storage should reduce the effort needed to put things away, not the effort needed to get them out.** When we use something, we have a clear purpose for getting it out. Unless for some reason it is incredibly hard work, we usually don't mind the effort involved. Clutter has only two possible causes: too much effort is required to put things away or it is unclear where things belong. If we overlook this vital point, we are likely to create a system that results in clutter. For people like me who are naturally lazy, I strongly recommend focusing storage in one spot. More often than not, the notion that it's more convenient to keep everything within arm's reach is a biased assumption.

Many people design their storage layout to match the flow plan within their house, but how do you think that flow plan developed in the first place? In almost every case, flow plan is determined not by what a person does during the day but by where he or she stores things. We may think that we have stored things to suit our behavior, but usually we have unconsciously adjusted our actions to match where things are stored. Laying out storage space to follow the current flow plan will only disperse storage throughout the house. That, in turn, will increase the chances that we will accumulate more possessions and forget what we already have, making life more difficult.

Considering the average size of a Japanese dwelling, a storage layout that follows the flow plan is not going to make that much difference. If it only takes ten to twenty seconds to walk from one end of your home to the other, do you really need to worry about flow plan? **If you are aiming for an uncluttered room, it is much more important to arrange your storage so that you can tell at a glance where everything is than to worry about the details of who does what, where, and when.**

There is no need to get complicated. Just designate where to keep your things in accordance with the design of your home and your storage problems will be solved. Your house already knows where things belong. This is why the storage method I use is so amazingly simple. To be frank, I can remember where everything is kept in almost all my clients' homes. That's how simple my method is. I have never considered the flow plan when helping clients organize, yet none of them has had any problems. On the contrary, once they've created a simple storage plan, they never have to ponder where something belongs; it becomes natural to put things away, and consequently, there is no more clutter in the home.

Store everything similar in the same place or in close proximity. Don't disperse your storage space. If you follow this advice, you will find that you have created a very natural flow plan. There is also no need whatsoever to consider frequency of use when designing storage space. Some books on tidying offer methods that classify things into six levels according to frequency of use: daily, once every three days, once a week, once a month, once a year, and less than once a year. Am I the only one whose head swims at the very thought of dividing my drawers into six compartments? At the most, I use only two categories for frequency of use: things I use often and things I don't.

Take the contents of a drawer, for example. You will naturally start keeping the things you use less in the back of the drawer and those you use more in the front. There is no need to decide this when you first lay out your storage space. **When you are choosing what to keep, ask your heart; when you are choosing where to store something, ask your house.** If you remember to do this, you will instinctively know how to proceed with organizing and storing your things.

Never pile things: vertical storage is the key

There are people who stack everything in piles, be it books, papers, or clothes. But this is a great waste. When it comes to storage, vertical is best. I am particularly obsessed with this point. I store every item vertically if possible, including clothes, which I fold and stand on edge in my drawers, and stockings, which I roll up and stand in a box. The same is true for stationery and writing tools: whether boxes of staples, measuring tapes, or erasers, I stand them on edge. I even store my laptop in the bookcase as if it were indeed a notebook. If you have storage space that should be sufficient yet falls short, try standing things vertically. You'll find that this solves most problems.

I store things vertically and avoid stacking for two reasons. First, if you stack things, you end up with what seems like inexhaustible storage space. Things can be stacked forever and endlessly on top, which makes it harder to notice the increasing volume. In contrast, when things are stored vertically, any increase takes up space and you will eventually run out of storage area. When you do, you'll notice, "Ah, I'm starting to accumulate stuff again."

The other reason is this: **stacking is very hard on the things at the bottom.** When things are piled on top of one another, the things underneath get squished. Stacking weakens and exhausts the things that bear the weight of the pile. Just imagine how you would feel if you were forced to carry a heavy load for hours. Not only that, but the things in the pile virtually disappear because we forget that they even exist. When we pile our clothes one on top of the other, the clothes at the bottom are used less and less frequently. The outfits that no longer thrill my clients even though they loved them at the time of purchase are very often the ones that spent a long time at the bottom of the pile.

This applies to papers and documents as well. As soon as another document is placed on top, the first document recedes a little further from our awareness, and before we know it, we put off dealing with it or even forget about it altogether. So for these reasons, I recommend storing vertically anything that can be stood up. Try taking a pile you already have and standing it up. Just by doing that you will become more aware of the volume of things in that pile. Vertical storage can be used anywhere. Messy fridges are common, but their contents can be organized quickly and simply by standing things on end. I happen to love carrots, for example. If you open my fridge, you'll find carrots standing in the drink holders on the door.

No need for commercial storage items

The world is full of handy storage items. Adjustable dividers, cloth racks that can be hung from the rod in your closet, narrow shelves that fit into small spaces. You can find storage items you never imagined existed at any store, from the local dollar shop to high-end fancy furniture and housewares stores. I was once a storage fanatic myself, so at one period, I tried just about every item there was on the market, including the weirdest and most exotic. Yet there are almost none left in my house.

The storage items you'll find in my house are several sets of clear plastic drawers for my clothes and *komono*, a set of cardboard drawers I have used since I was in junior high school, and a rattan basket for my towels. That's it.

And all of them are kept inside the built-in closet. Other than these, there are the built-in shelves in the kitchen and washroom and the shoe cupboard in the entranceway. I don't need a bookcase because I store my books and papers on one of the shelves in the shoe cupboard. The built-in closets and shelves, far from being large, are smaller than average. Basically, the only storage items you need are plain old drawers and boxes—you don't need anything special or fancy.

People often ask me what I recommend, no doubt expecting me to reveal some hitherto secret storage weapon. But I can tell you right now: there is no need to buy dividers or any other gadget. You can solve your storage problems with things you already have in the house. The most common item I use is an empty shoebox. I have tried all kinds of storage products, but have never found any other that is free and still surpasses the shoebox. It gets above average marks for all five of my criteria: size, material, durability, ease of use, and attractiveness. These well-balanced attributes and its versatility are its greatest merits. Shoes come in boxes with cute designs as well. I frequently ask my clients, "Do you have any shoeboxes?" when I visit their homes.

Shoeboxes have infinite uses. I commonly use them to store socks and stockings in drawers. Shoebox height is perfect for standing up rolled stockings. In the washroom, they can be used to store bottles of shampoo, conditioner, etc., and they're also perfect for holding detergents and other household cleaning items. In the kitchen, they can be used to stock foodstuffs as well as garbage bags, cloths, and so on. I also use them to hold cake pans, pie plates, and other cooking items that get less frequent use. The box can then be stored on an upper shelf. For some reason, many people seem to store their baking pans in plastic bags, but they are much easier to use when stored in a shoebox. This extremely easy solution is very popular with my clients. I am always pleased when they tell me that they bake more often since reorganizing.

The lid of a shoebox is shallow and can be used like a tray. It can be placed in the cupboard to hold your cooking oils and spices, keeping the base of the cupboard clean. Unlike many shelf liners, these lids don't slip and are much easier to replace. If you keep cooking utensils such as your ladle and spatula in the kitchen drawers, you can use the shoebox lid to hold them. This keeps the utensils from rolling about noisily in the drawer every time you open and close it, and because it acts as a divider, you can use the remaining space more effectively.

Of course, there are many other types of boxes that make handy storage items. Those that I use most frequently include the plastic cases that hold business cards and those that come with portable music players made by Apple. In fact, the boxes that contain many Apple products are the right size and design for storage, so if you have any, I recommend using them as dividers in your drawers. They are perfect for storing writing tools.

Another standard item is extra plastic food containers, which can be used to store small items in the kitchen.

Basically, any square box or container of the right size will do. Large cardboard boxes or electrical appliance boxes, however, are too big for storage dividers, inconvenient for other types of storage, and just plain ugly. Please get rid of them. Whenever you come across likely storage boxes while you are cleaning and sorting your belongings, set them aside in one spot until you are ready to start storing. Be sure to discard or recycle any that are left once your house is in order. Never hang on to them in the belief that you might use them someday.

I don't recommend using round, heart-shaped, or irregularly shaped containers as dividers because they usually waste space. However, if a particular box gives you a thrill when you hold it, that's different. To discard it or to keep it without using it would be a waste, so here you should follow your intuition and use it for storage. You can, for example, use such boxes in a drawer for hair accessories, or to store cotton swabs or your sewing kit. Create your own original combinations by matching an empty box to fit an item that needs storing. The best method is to experiment and enjoy the process.

When my clients use what they already have in the house like this, they always find that they have exactly what they need to store their things. They don't need to go out and buy storage items. Of course, there are plenty of great designer items out there. But right now, the important thing is to finish putting your house in order as soon as possible. **Rather than buying something to make do for now, wait until you have completed the entire process and then take your time looking for storage items that you really like.**

The best way to store bags is in another bag

Handbags, purses, and other bags that are not in use are empty. At one point in this business, it struck me that this was a great waste of space, especially as they are often kept in prime storage locations. Not only do they take up more room because they can't be folded, but also they are often stuffed with tissue paper to keep their shape. In Japanese homes where storage is extremely limited, this seemed like an unpardonably extravagant use of space. The fact that the tissue paper often starts to shred just adds insult to injury.

Determined to find a solution, I began to experiment. First, I decided to do away with the tissue paper. After all, getting rid of things that don't spark joy is key to the KonMari Method. Instead, I tried stuffing the bag with small off-season items. In summer, I used scarves and mittens, and in winter, I used items such as bathing suits. The bags not only kept their shape but also doubled as storage space. I was delighted to find a solution that seemed to kill two birds with one stone. But within a year, I had abandoned this approach. Although in theory it seemed like a great idea, in practice, having to remove the items every time I wanted to use a handbag was a pain, and once removed, those items cluttered up the closet.

Of course, I did not give up. I kept looking for some kind of stuffing that would not shred. My next idea was to put small items in a thin cloth bag first before filling the purse. Removal was easy and the cloth bag actually looked nice even when exposed in the cupboard. I was pleased to have discovered yet another groundbreaking solution. But this method, too, had a hidden drawback. I could not see the off-season items inside, and when their season came around, I completely forgot to empty two of the inner bags. It wasn't until a year later that I finally noticed them, and by then, their contents were looking very forlorn. This made me pause for thought. Despite the fact that my policy for clothes and other items is to keep off-season things in sight, I had foolishly believed that I would remember to take out what I could not see.

I emptied out the cloth bags and freed the items inside, but the handbags they had been supporting now looked wilted. I needed something to help them keep their shape, but I certainly didn't want to fill them with off-season clothes that I would likely forget. Not knowing what to do, I decided to place one bag inside another just for the time being. This, in fact, turned out to be the perfect solution.

By storing bags inside each other, I halved the amount of storage space needed, and I could keep track of their contents by letting the straps dangle outside.

The key is to put the same type of bags together. Sets should consist of handbags made from similar material, such as stiff leather or thickly woven cloth, or of purses for special occasions, such as weddings and funerals. Dividing by material and/or by type of use means that you only need to take out one set whenever you need a handbag. This is much easier. Keep in mind, however, that you should not store too many handbags in one. My rule of thumb is to keep no more than two in any one bag and to make sure that I store them so that I won't forget what's inside. In the case of knapsacks, which fold up surprisingly small, I recommend storing them all inside a single knapsack.

To summarize, the best way to store purses, handbags, and other bags is to make sets according to the material, size, and frequency of use and to store them one inside the other, like nested boxes. All straps and handles should be left in plain view. If the handbag used for storage came in a bag, you can store the set in that. Line up these sets in your closet or wardrobe where you can see them. I stand them on the top shelf . The process of storing bags inside another bag, of finding the right combinations, is a lot of fun, much like making a jigsaw puzzle. When you find just the right pair, where the outer and inner bags fit so well together that they support one another, it is like witnessing a meeting that was destined to be.

Empty your bag every day

There are some things you need on a daily basis, such as your wallet, your bus or train pass, and your date book. Many people see no point in taking these things out when they come home because they will use them again the next day, but this is a mistake. The purpose of a purse or messenger bag is to carry your things for you when you're away from home. You fill your bag with the things you need, such as documents, your cell phone, and your wallet, and it carries them all without complaint, even if it is filled to bursting. When you put it down and it scrapes its bottom on the floor, it utters no word of criticism, only doing its best to support you. What a hard worker! It would be cruel not to give it a break at least at home. Being packed all the time, even when not in use, must feel something like going to bed on a full stomach. If you treat your handbags like this, they will soon look tired and worn.

If you do not make a habit of unpacking your bag, you are also quite likely to leave something inside when you decide to use another bag, and before you know it, you will have forgotten what you have in each one. Unable to find a pen or lip balm, you will wind up buying a new one. The most common items found in my clients' handbags when we tidy up their rooms are tissues, coins, crumpled receipts, and used chewing gum wadded in its wrapper. There is a real danger that important items like accessories, memo pads, or documents may become mixed up with these.

So, empty your bag every day. This is not as bothersome as it sounds. You just need to make a place for the things inside it. Find a box and place your train pass, company ID, and other important items vertically inside it. Then put the box just like that into a drawer or cupboard. Any box will do, but if you can't find the right size, a shoebox will work fine. Or you can make a space in one corner of a drawer, without using a box at all. Appearance is important, so if you're using a box, don't hesitate to look for one that you really like. One of the best places to keep this box is on top of the set of drawers you use for storage, and it is more convenient if that is close to where you keep your bag.

If you can't empty your bag sometimes, that's all right. There are times when I come home very late at night that I don't bother to empty my bag because I plan to use it again for work early the next morning. Just between you and me, while writing this book, there have been times when I came home and fell asleep on the floor without even changing my clothes. The important thing is to create an environment where your bag can have a rest by designating a specific place to store everything you usually carry inside it.

Items that usurp floor space belong in the closet

If you have built-in closets in your home, most of the things in your house can be stored inside them. Japanese closets are ideal storage spaces. They are deep and wide, are divided into top and bottom by a broad and extremely sturdy shelf, and have a cupboard built into the wall above. But many Japanese people do not know how to take advantage of this space. For those of you who have closets like this, the best policy is to use these faithfully. No matter how hard you might try to design some ingenious device to solve all your storage problems, the end result is almost always more difficult to use than what is already there.

The basic method for effective use of a closet is as follows. First, as a general rule, off-season items should be stored in the cupboard above the closet. This includes seasonal ornaments, skiwear, and hiking or other seasonal sportswear and goods. This is also the best spot for large mementos that will not fit in a bookcase, such as a wedding album or photo albums. But don't put them in cardboard boxes. Instead, stand them up toward the front of the cupboard as you would books in a bookcase. Otherwise, you are unlikely to ever see them again.

Regular clothes should be stored in the closet. If you use clear plastic cases to store them, I strongly recommend the drawer rather than the box type. The instant clothes are put away in a box, they become a pain to remove, and in most cases, people never bother to take them out even when they are back in season. And, of course, fold and stand the clothes on edge in the drawer.

Bedding is best stored on the upper shelf of the closet where it is less exposed to humidity and dust. The bottom space can be used to store electrical appliances such as fans and space heaters during the off-season. The best way to use a Japanese-style closet is to think of it as a small room and to store the things inside it in drawers or other storage units. I had one client who kept all her clothes loose in the closet. When we opened the door, it looked like a garbage dump and the clothes resembled a tangled mess of noodles.

It is far more efficient to move all your storage units into your closet. This is where I usually put steel racks, bookcases, and plywood cupboards or shelves, which can also be used to store books. I also store any large items that take up floor space, such as suitcases, golf clubs, electrical appliances, or guitars, in the closet. I'm sure many of my clients did not believe they could ever fit all their things into their closet, but once they followed my method for thoroughly sorting and discarding, it was quite simple.

Keep things out of the bath and the kitchen sink

How many bottles of shampoo and conditioner line your bathtub? Different family members may use different products, or you may have several kinds that you use depending on your mood or for once-a-week treatments. But these are such a bother to move when you clean the bath. Kept on the floor in the shower or on the edge of the bath, they become slimy. To avoid this, some people use a wire basket as a container, but from my own experience, this makes things even worse.

I once bought a wire basket big enough to fit all the soaps, shampoos, and even facial masks used by my family. My delight at this convenient item was short-lived. At first, I dried it every time I had a bath, but soon wiping every wire became a chore and I did it only once every three days, then every five days, then even less, until I had completely forgotten to take care of it. One day, I noticed that the shampoo bottle was red and slimy on the bottom. Examining the rack, I saw that it was so covered in slime I could not bear to look at it. Almost in tears, I scrubbed the wire rack clean and not long after got rid of it. It was just too much trouble and every time I got in the bath and saw it, it reminded me of that disgusting slime episode. I should have realized that the bath is the most humid place in the house, which obviously makes it the most unsuitable place for storing anything.

There is no need to keep soaps and shampoos out when we are not using them, and the added exposure to heat and moisture when they aren't in use is bound to affect their quality. It is therefore my policy to keep everything out of the bath or shower. Whatever is used in the bath should be dried after use anyway, so it makes far more sense to just wipe down the few items we use with our bath towel and then put them away in the cupboard. While this may seem like more work at first glance, it is actually less. It is much quicker and easier to clean the bath or shower without these items cluttering that space, and there will be less slime buildup.

The same is true for the kitchen sink area. Do you keep your sponges and dish detergent by the sink? I store mine underneath it. The secret is to make sure the sponge is completely dry. Many people use a wire sponge rack with suction cups that stick to the sink. If you do, too, I recommend that you remove it immediately. It cannot dry out if it is sprayed with water every time you use the sink, and it will soon start to smell. To prevent this, squeeze your sponge tightly after use and hang it up to dry. You can use a clothespin to pin it to your towel rack or to the handle of a kitchen drawer if you don't have a rack. Personally, I recommend hanging sponges outside, such as on the veranda.

I dry not only my sponges but also my cutting boards, colanders, and dishes on my veranda. Sunlight is a good disinfectant, and my kitchen always looks very tidy because I don't need a dish rack. In fact, I don't even own a dish rack. I put all the dishes I wash into a large bowl or colander and place this on the veranda to dry. I can wash them in the morning and just leave them outside. This is an excellent solution for people living on their own or for those who don't use many dishes.

Where do you store your oil, salt, pepper, soy sauce, and other seasonings? Many people keep them right beside the stove because they want them close at hand for the sake of convenience. If you are one of these people, I hope you will rescue them right now. For one thing, a counter is for preparing food, not for storing things. Counter space beside the stove, in particular, is exposed to splatters of food and oil, and the seasonings kept here are usually sticky with grease. Rows of bottles in this area also make it much harder to keep clean, and the kitchen area will always be covered in a film of oil. Kitchen shelves and cupboards are usually designed to store seasonings and spices, so put them away where they belong. Quite often, a long, narrow drawer is located next to the oven that can be used for this purpose.

Make the top shelf of the bookcase your personal shrine

I once worked as a Shinto shrine maiden for five years. I have loved shrines since I was in grade school and would often drop by our community shrine to pay my respects to the local deity. Even people who don't love shrines as I do still have protective talismans and good-luck charms in their homes. I have found countless charms from shrines all over Japan, such as Izumo Taisha, in my clients' homes. The people I meet not only work hard to refine both body and mind but also remember to ask the gods for extra luck. While this is commendable, my clients have more than enough charms to spare.

Please keep in mind that charms are not something you buy but something with which you are entrusted. They are effective only for one year after you receive them, so those that are past their expiration dates should be returned as soon as possible. You do not need to take a charm back to the same place you bought it, but do remember that Shinto charms should be taken to a shrine and Buddhist charms to a temple.

What should be done with charms and talismans that are still effective? They are actually intended to be carried on your person, by attaching them to your key ring, putting them in your purse, or clipping them to the metal rings if you use a refillable date book. But there is a limit to how many you can carry like this, and if you visit several temples and shrines a year, you may have quite a collection. To carry them all around with you is pretentious, and having too many will not inspire joy in anyone. One of my clients was a thirty-one-year-old woman who worked for a foreign consulting firm. Like many other Japanese women, she enjoyed having her fortune told and visiting power spots. Her house was filled with charms she had collected over the years. They emerged from such places as a box kept deep in a desk drawer and from between the pages of her books. Altogether we found thirty-four charms, including one given to her by her grandmother for success in her studies and several talismans from shrines famous for romance. Many had expired. In addition, she had a mini Buddha from India, a mini Virgin Mary from Europe, and various crystals and other power stones.

In cases like this, I recommend that my clients make a personal altar in a corner of their house. Although I use the word "altar," there is no need to worry about the direction it faces or the design. Just make a corner that is shrine-like. I recommend the top shelf in a bookcase because locating it above eye level makes it more shrine-like. **One theme underlying my method of tidying is transforming the home into a sacred space, a power spot filled with pure energy.** A comfortable environment, a space that feels good to be in, a place where you can relax—these are the traits that make a home a power spot. Would you rather live in a home like this or in one that resembles a storage shed? The answer, I hope, is obvious.

Decorate your closet with your secret delights

"Don't open that, please!" is a common refrain. My clients usually have a drawer, a box, or a closet that they don't want to show me. We all have things that we would rather other people didn't know about us, yet which we feel are important. Common items in this category are posters of pop idols and other fan memorabilia, and hobby-related books. The posters are often rolled up in the back of the closet and CDs stowed in a box. But this is a waste. Your room at least should be the one place where you can pursue and enjoy your interests to your heart's content. So if you like something, don't hide it away. If you want to enjoy them but don't want your friends or others to know, I have a solution. **Transform your closet into your own private space, one that gives you a thrill of pleasure.** Use these treasures to decorate the back wall of the closet behind your clothes or the inside of the door.

You can decorate your closet with anything, whether private or not. Use posters, photos, ornaments, whatever you like. There are no limits on how to decorate your storage space. No one will complain and no one will see. Your storage space is your private paradise, so personalize it to the fullest.

Unpack and de-tag new clothes immediately

One of the many things that amazes me when I help my clients tidy is the number of items that are still in their packages. Food and sanitary items I can understand, but why do people shove clothes such as socks and underwear in their drawer without removing them from the package? They take up more space that way and are also more likely to be forgotten.

My father liked to stock up on socks. Every time he went to the supermarket, he would buy gray or black socks to wear with his suits and store them in their packages in his drawer. Gray sweaters were another item he liked to keep on hand, and I often came across them in the back of the closet, still wrapped in their plastic packages. I always felt rather sorry for these clothes. I had thought this habit was unique to my father, but when I started visiting my clients' homes, I realized that there are many people like him. The stock usually consists of something the client regularly wears, the most common being consumables such as socks, underwear, and stockings. The one thing these clients have in common is that they have far more stock than they need. I was astounded to find that they buy more of the same item before they have unpacked those previously purchased. Perhaps the fact that they are in packages dulls the person's sense of ownership. The record number of stockings I discovered in a client's house, for example, was eighty-two pairs. Still in their packages, they filled up an entire plastic storage case.

Granted, when you buy something, it is easiest to just throw it into your drawer still packaged. And perhaps there is some pleasure in ripping off the wrapper when you first wear it. But the only difference between packaged goods in your drawer and those in the store is the place where they are kept. People commonly assume that it is cheaper to buy things in bulk when on sale. But I believe the opposite is true. If you consider the cost of storage, it is just as economical to keep these things in the store, not in your home. Moreover, if you buy and use them as you need them, they will be newer and in better condition. This is why I urge you to refrain from stocking up on things. Instead, buy only what you need, remove all items from their packages immediately, and put them away. If you already have a large stock of something, at least remove them from their packages. Being left in the package does clothes nothing but harm.

The most common item to be left in the package is stockings. When you remove them, take out the stiff liner, too. You won't need that at home. **Stockings take up 25 percent less room once they are out of the package and folded up.** They are also far more likely to be used this way because they are easier to get at. I think it is only when you have removed something from the package that you can really call it your own.

Similar to clothes in the package are those with the tags still on. I frequently find skirts or cardigans in my clients' homes with the price tags or brand name still on them. In most cases, the client has forgotten their existence and looks surprised to see them, despite the fact that these items have been hanging in plain sight in their closet. For a long time, I wondered what makes such clothes invisible. Determined to find an explanation, I went to observe the clothing sections in various department stores.

After continuing my research for some time, I realized that there is a noticeable difference between clothes in someone's closet and those hanging on a rack in a store. The latter have a very different aura from the hardworking clothes we use every day. They exude a crisp primness, and clothes with their price tags still on retain that primness. This is how I see it: clothes in a store are products, whereas clothes in the home are personal possessions. Clothes that still have their price tag on have not yet been made our own and therefore they don't quite "belong." Overpowered by the aura of our "legitimate" clothes, they are less noticeable. It is only natural that we overlook and eventually even forget them as we look through our wardrobe.

Some people worry that if they remove the tags their value will drop if they ever take them to a recycle shop, but that is a contradiction. If you are going to buy clothes, choose them with the intention of welcoming them into your home and caring for them. When you buy them, remove the tags immediately. In order for your clothes to make the transition from store products to personal possessions, you need to perform the ritual of cutting the "umbilical cord" that links them to the shop.

Don't underestimate the "noise" of written information

Advanced students generally demand an even higher level of comfort in their space once they have successfully resolved the issues of excessive belongings and storage. At first glance, the homes of some of my clients are so uncluttered that they do not even appear to need my assistance.

One such client was a woman in her thirties who lived with her husband and their six-year-old daughter. She had no qualms about discarding, and at our first lesson she got rid of two hundred books and thirty-two bags of garbage. She was primarily a homemaker and spent her time taking care of the house, hosting teas for other mothers with children twice a month, and holding regular flower-arranging classes in her home. She had frequent visitors and was quite conscious about keeping her home tidy so that she would not feel embarrassed to receive surprise guests. She lived in a two-bedroom home with a combined dining room and kitchen, and their belongings fit neatly into the built-in closets and two head-height wire racks. The plain wood floors were bare and always well polished. Her friends wondered how she could be tidier than she already was, but she still seemed discontent.

"We don't have a lot of things, but somehow I just don't feel settled. I feel like there's one more step I need to take."

When I visited her house, it was tidy, but just as she had said, something didn't feel quite right. The first thing I do at times like this is open the doors of all the storage areas. When I opened the main closet, I found what I had been expecting. Labels proclaiming "Great Storage Solutions!" were stuck to the clear plastic drawers, packages of room deodorizers were emblazoned with "Freshens Air Instantly!" and the cardboard boxes announced "Iyo Oranges." Everywhere I looked, words, words, and more words leaped out at me. Here was the last "step" my client was seeking. A deluge of information whenever you open a closet door makes a room feel "noisy." Particularly if the words are in your own language, they jump into your line of vision, and your brain treats them as information to be sorted. This creates commotion in your mind.

In the case of my client, every time she wanted to choose her clothes, she was assailed by such messages as "Iyo Oranges" and "Freshens Air Instantly!" almost as if someone were muttering constantly in her ear. Strangely, just closing the cupboard doors does not conceal the flood of information. The words become static that fills the air. From my own experience, the storage spaces of homes that feel "noisy" even though they look very neat on the surface usually are overflowing with unnecessary information. The neater the house and the more sparse its furnishings, the louder this information feels. So start by removing the product seals from your storage containers. This is absolutely essential, just as you remove the tags from new clothes to welcome them as your personal belongings. Tear the printed film off packages that you don't want to see, such as deodorizers and detergents. Spaces that are out of sight are still part of your house. **By eliminating excess visual information that doesn't inspire joy, you can make your space much more peaceful and comfortable.** The difference this makes is so amazing it would be a waste not to try it.

Appreciate your possessions and gain strong allies

One of the homework assignments I give my clients is to **appreciate their belongings.** For example, I urge them to try saying, "Thank you for keeping me warm all day," when they hang up their clothes after returning home. Or, when removing their accessories, I suggest they say, "Thank you for making me beautiful," and when putting their bag in the closet, to say, "It's thanks to you that I got so much work done today." Express your appreciation to every item that supported you during the day. If you find this hard to do daily, then at least do it whenever you can.

I began to treat my belongings as if they were alive when I was a high school student. I had my own cell phone. Although the screen was still monochrome, I loved the compact design and pale blue color. I was not an addicted user, but I liked my phone so much that I broke the school rules and slipped it into the pocket of my school uniform every day. I would take it out occasionally to admire it and smile to myself. Technology progressed and everyone was getting cell phones with color screens. I hung on to my outdated model as long as I could, but finally it had become too scratched and worn, and I had to replace it. When I got my new cell phone, I hit upon the idea of texting my old phone. It was my first replacement and I was probably feeling quite excited. After thinking for a moment, I typed the simple message "Thank you for everything" and added a heart symbol. Then I pressed SEND. My old phone pinged immediately and I checked my texts. Of course it was the message I had just sent. "Great. My message reached you. I really wanted to say thanks for all you have done," I said to my old phone. Then I closed it with a click.

A few minutes later, I opened my old phone and was surprised to find that the screen was blank. No matter which button I pressed, the screen did not respond. My cell phone, which had never broken since the day I first got it, had gone dead after receiving my message. It never worked again, as if the phone, realizing that its job was done, had resigned from its post of its own accord.

Of course, I know some people find it hard to believe that inanimate objects respond to human emotion, and it could indeed just have been coincidence. Still, we often hear about athletes who take loving care of their sports gear, treating it almost as if it were sacred. I think the athletes instinctively sense the power of these objects. If we treated all things we use in our daily life, whether it is our computer, our handbag, or our pens and pencils, with the same care that athletes give to their equipment, we could greatly increase the number of dependable "supporters" in our lives. The act of possessing is a very natural part of our daily life, not something reserved for some special match or contest.

Even if we remain unaware of it, our belongings really work hard for us, carrying out their respective roles each day to support our lives. Just as we like to come home and relax after a day's work, our things breathe a sigh of relief when they return to where they belong. Have you ever thought about what it would be like to have no fixed address? Our lives would be very uncertain. It is precisely because we have a home to return to that we can go out to work, to shop, or to interact with others. The same is true for our belongings. It is important for them to have that same reassurance that there is a place for them to return to. You can tell the difference. Possessions that have a place where they belong and to which they are returned each day for a rest are more vibrant.

Once my clients have learned to treat their clothes with respect, they always tell me, "My clothes last longer. My sweaters don't pill as easily, and I don't spill things on them as much either." This suggests that caring for your possessions is the best way to motivate them to support you, their owner. When you treat your belongings well, they will always respond in kind. For this reason, I take time to ask myself occasionally whether the storage space I've set aside for them will make them happy. Storage, after all, is the sacred act of choosing a home for my belongings.

5

—

The magic of tidying dramatically transforms your life

Put your house in order and discover what you really want to do

In Japan, the image of a class representative is someone who is popular, has leadership qualities, and likes to stand out, and we use the term "class-rep type" for anyone with these qualities. In contrast, I am the "organizer type," an eccentric who works away quietly and unobtrusively in the corner of the classroom, organizing the shelves. I mean this literally and quite seriously.

The first official task I was given in elementary school was "tidying." I can vividly recall that day. Everyone was vying for jobs like feeding the school pets or watering the plants, but when the teacher said, "Who would like to be responsible for organizing and tidying the classroom?" no one raised their hand but me, and I did so with great enthusiasm. In retrospect, my tidying genes were already activated even at that early age. From previous chapters, you already know how I spent my days at school, happily and confidently reorganizing the classroom, lockers, and bookshelves.

When I share this story, people often say, "You're so lucky you knew what you liked at such a young age. I'm jealous. I have no idea what I'd like to do. . . ." But I actually only realized quite recently how much I like organizing. Although I spend almost all my time involved in tidying, either teaching my clients in their homes or giving lectures, when I was young, my dream was to get married. Tidying was such an integral part of my daily life that it wasn't until the day I started my own business that I realized it could be my profession. When people asked me what I liked to do, I would hesitate and then finally say in desperation, "Read books," all the while wondering, "What do I like to do?" I completely forgot about being assigned the role of class organizer in grade school. Fifteen years later, I had a sudden flashback while tidying my room. In my mind, I could see my teacher writing my name on the blackboard and realized with surprise that I had been interested in this field since I was very young.

Think back to your own school days and the things you enjoyed doing. Perhaps you were responsible for feeding the pets or maybe you liked drawing pictures. Whatever it was, the chances are that it is related in some way to something that you are doing now, as a natural part of your life, even if you are not doing it in the same way. **At their core, the things we really like do not change over time. Putting your house in order is a great way to discover what they are.**

One of my clients has been a good friend of mine since college. Although she originally worked for a major IT company after graduating, she discovered what she really likes doing through tidying. When we finished putting her house in order, she looked at her bookcase, which now contained only those books that captivated her, and realized that the titles were all related to social welfare. The many books she had bought to study English or hone her computer skills after entering the workforce were gone, while those on social welfare, which she had bought as a junior high school student, remained. Looking at them, she was reminded of the volunteer work she had done as a babysitter for many years before entering the company. Suddenly she realized that she wanted to contribute to building a society where parents could work without feeling anxious about their kids. Aware for the first time of her passion, she spent the year after my course studying and preparing, then quit her job and started a child care company. She now has many clients who rely on her services and enjoys each day to the fullest as she explores how to further improve her business.

"When I put my house in order, I discovered what I really wanted to do." These are words I hear frequently from my clients. For the majority, the experience of tidying causes them to become more passionately involved in their work. Some set up their own companies, others change jobs, and still others take more interest in their current profession. They also become more passionate about their other interests and about their home and family life. Their awareness of what they like naturally increases and, as a result, daily life becomes more exciting.

Although we can get to know ourselves better by sitting down and analyzing our characteristics or by listening to others' perspectives on us, I believe that tidying is the best way. After all, our possessions very accurately relate the history of the decisions we have made in life. Tidying is a way of taking stock that shows us what we really like.

The magic effect of tidying

"Up to now, I believed it was important to do things that added to my life, so I took seminars and studied to increase my knowledge. But through your course on how to put my space in order, I realized for the first time that **letting go is even more important than adding.**"

This comment was made by a client in her thirties who loved to study and who had developed a vast network of contacts. Her life changed drastically after she took my course. The primary item she did not want to part with was her enormous collection of seminar notes and materials, but when she finally disposed of them, she felt as if a huge weight had been lifted from her. After getting rid of almost five hundred books she had been intending to read someday, she found that she received new information daily. And when she discarded her huge stack of business cards, the people that she had been wanting to meet started calling her and she was able to meet them quite naturally. Whereas before she had been into spirituality, when the course concluded she said contentedly, "Tidying has far more effect than feng shui or power stones and other spiritual goods." Since then, she has leaped headlong into a new life, quitting her job and finding a publisher for her book.

Tidying dramatically changes one's life. This is true for everyone, 100 percent. The impact of this effect, which I have dubbed "the magic of tidying," is phenomenal. Sometimes I ask my clients how their lives changed after taking the course. Although I have grown accustomed to their answers, in the beginning even I was surprised. **The lives of those who tidy thoroughly and completely, in a single shot, are without exception dramatically altered.**

The client I just described had been messy all her life. When her mother saw her room clutter-free, she was so impressed that she signed up for my course, too. Although she believed herself to be a tidy person, the sight of her daughter's room convinced her that she was not. She came to enjoy discarding so much that she had no regrets about getting rid of her tea ceremony equipment, which had cost $250, and looked forward eagerly to trash and recycle pickup days.

"Previously, I had no confidence. I kept thinking that I needed to change, that I should be different, but now I can believe that I am okay just the way I am. By gaining a clear standard by which I can judge things, I gained a great deal of confidence in myself." As you can see from her testimony, **one of the magical effects of tidying is confidence in your decision-making capacity.** Tidying means taking each item in your hand, asking yourself whether it sparks joy, and deciding on this basis whether or not to keep it. By repeating this process hundreds and thousands of times, we naturally hone our decision-making skills. People who lack confidence in their judgment lack confidence in themselves. I, too, once lacked confidence. What saved me was tidying.

Gaining confidence in life through the magic of tidying

I have come to the conclusion that my passion for tidying was motivated by a desire for recognition from my parents and a complex concerning my mother. Being the middle child of three siblings, I did not get much attention from my parents after the age of three. Of course, this was not intentional, but being sandwiched between my older brother and the youngest child, my little sister, I could not help but feel this way.

My interest in housework and tidying began when I was about five, and I believe that I was trying in my own way not to make trouble for my parents, who were clearly busy taking care of my other two siblings. I also became conscious from a very young age of the need to avoid being dependent on other people. And, of course, I wanted my parents to praise and notice me.

From the time I was a first grader, I used an alarm clock to wake up before everyone else. I did not like being dependent on others, found it hard to trust them, and was very inept at expressing my feelings. From the fact that I spent my recesses alone, tidying, you can guess that I wasn't a very outgoing child. I really enjoyed wandering around the school by myself, and I still prefer to do things alone, including traveling and shopping. This is very natural for me.

Because I was poor at developing bonds of trust with people, I had an unusually strong attachment to things. I think that precisely because I did not feel comfortable exposing my weaknesses or my true feelings to others, my room and the things in it became very precious. I did not have to pretend or hide anything in front of them. It was material things and my house that taught me to appreciate unconditional love first, not my parents or friends. To tell the truth, I still don't have a lot of self-confidence. There are times when I am quite discouraged by my inadequacies.

I do, however, have confidence in my environment. When it comes to the things I own, the clothes I wear, the house I live in, and the people in my life, when it comes to my environment as a whole, although it may not seem particularly special to anyone else, I am confident and extremely grateful to be surrounded by what I love, by things and people that are, each and every one, special, precious, and exceedingly dear to me. The things and people that bring me joy support me. They give me the confidence that I will be all right. I want to help others who feel the way I once did, who lack self-confidence and find it hard to open their hearts to others, to see how much support they receive from the space they live in and the things that surround them. This is why I spend my time visiting people's homes and instructing them in how to tidy.

An attachment to the past or anxiety about the future

"Discard anything that doesn't spark joy." If you have tried this method even a little, you have realized by now that it is not that difficult to identify something that brings you joy. The moment you touch it, you know the answer. It is much more difficult to decide to discard something. We come up with all kinds of reasons for not doing it, such as "I didn't use this particular pot all year, but who knows, I might need it sometime. . . ." or "That necklace my boyfriend gave me, I really liked it at the time. . . ." **But when we really delve into the reasons for why we can't let something go, there are only two: an attachment to the past or a fear for the future.**

During the selection process, if you come across something that does not spark joy but that you just can't bring yourself to throw away, stop a moment and ask yourself, "Am I having trouble getting rid of this because of an attachment to the past or because of a fear for the future?" Ask this for every one of these items. As you do so, you'll begin to see a pattern in your ownership of things, a pattern that falls into one of three categories: attachment to the past, desire for stability in the future, or a combination of both. It's important to understand your ownership pattern because it is an expression of the values that guide your life. **The question of what you want to own is actually the question of how you want to live your life.** Attachment to the past and fears concerning the future not only govern the way you select the things you own but also represent the criteria by which you make choices in every aspect of your life, including your relationships with people and your job.

When a woman who is very anxious about the future chooses a partner, for example, she is less likely to select someone purely because she likes and enjoys being with him. She might choose someone she doesn't really like simply because the relationship seems advantageous to her or because she is afraid that if she doesn't choose him, she may not find anyone else. When it comes to career choices, the same type of person is more likely to choose a job with a large company because it will give her more choices in the future, or to work toward certain qualifications as a guarantee rather than because she actually likes the work and wants to do it. A person who has a strong attachment to the past, on the other hand, finds it hard to move on to a new relationship because she can't forget the boyfriend she broke up with two years ago. She also finds it hard to try out new methods even when the current method is no longer effective because it worked up to this point.

When one or the other of these thought patterns makes it hard to throw things away, we can't see what we really need now, at this moment. We aren't sure what would satisfy us or what we are looking for. As a result, we increase the number of unnecessary possessions, burying ourselves both physically and mentally in superfluous things. The best way to find out what we really need is to get rid of what we don't. Quests to faraway places or shopping sprees are no longer necessary. All you have to do is eliminate what you don't need by confronting each of your possessions properly.

The process of facing and selecting our possessions can be quite painful. It forces us to confront our imperfections and inadequacies and the foolish choices we made in the past. Many times when confronting my past during the tidying process, I have been so ashamed I felt like my face was on fire. My collection of scented erasers from grade school, the animation-related trinkets that I collected in junior high school, clothes I bought in high school when I was trying to act grown-up but that didn't suit me at all, handbags I bought even though I didn't need them just because I liked the look of them in the shop. The things we own are real. They exist here and now as a result of choices made in the past by no one other than ourselves. It is dangerous to ignore them or to discard them indiscriminately as if denying the choices we made. This is why I am against both letting things pile up and dumping things indiscriminately. It is only when we face the things we own one by one and experience the emotions they evoke that we can truly appreciate our relationship with them.

There are three approaches we can take toward our possessions: face them now, face them sometime, or avoid them until the day we die. The choice is ours. But I personally believe it is far better to face them now. If we acknowledge our attachment to the past and our fears for the future by honestly looking at our possessions, we will be able to see what is really important to us. This process in turn helps us identify our values and reduces doubt and confusion in making life decisions. If we can have confidence in our decisions and launch enthusiastically into action without any doubts holding us back, we will be able to achieve much more. In other words, the sooner we confront our possessions the better. If you are going to put your house in order, do it now.

Learning that you can do without

Once people get down to really tidying, they produce bag after bag of garbage. I have heard that the participants in my courses often compare notes on how many bags they have thrown away or share reports on what turned up in their house. The record number of garbage bags filled to date was by a couple who disposed of two hundred bags' worth of stuff, plus more than ten items that were too large to put in bags. Most people laugh when they hear this and imagine that the couple must have had a very large house with lots of storage room, but they are wrong. They lived in a very ordinary two-story, four-room dwelling. It had slightly more floor area than many Japanese homes because it also had an attic, but the difference in space was not that great. Although there did seem to be a lot of things in view, the home did not appear at first glance to have that much garbage in it. In other words, any house has the potential to produce the same volume.

When I have my clients sort through and get rid of their belongings, I don't stop halfway. The average amount discarded by a single person is easily twenty to thirty 45-liter bags, and for a family of three it's closer to seventy bags. **The sum total of all the garbage so far would exceed twenty-eight thousand bags, and the number of items discarded must be over one million.** Yet despite the drastic reduction in their belongings, no one has ever complained that they had a problem later because I told them to get rid of something. The reason is very clear: discarding those things that don't spark joy has no adverse effects whatsoever. When they finish tidying, all of my clients are surprised that they notice no inconvenience in their daily lives. It is a strong reminder that they have been living all this time surrounded by things that they don't need. There are no exceptions. Even clients who have less than a fifth of their possessions left at the end feel this way.

Of course, I am not saying that my clients have never regretted discarding something. Far from it. You should expect this to happen at least three times during the tidying process, but don't let it worry you. Even though my clients have regretted parting with something, they never complain. They have already learned through experience that any problem caused by lack of something can be solved through action. When my clients relate the experience of getting rid of something they shouldn't have, they all sound extremely cheerful. Most of them laugh and say, "For a moment I thought I was in trouble, but then I realized it wasn't life threatening." This attitude does not stem from an optimistic personality nor does it mean they have become careless in their response to missing something. Rather, it shows that by selecting what to discard, they have changed their mind-set.

What if, for example, they need the contents of a document that they disposed of earlier? First, because they have already pared down the amount of documents they own, they can quickly confirm that they do not have it, without having to search all over. **The fact that they do not need to search is actually an invaluable stress reliever.** One of the reasons clutter eats away at us is because we have to search for something just to find out whether it's even there, and many times, no matter how much we search, we cannot seem to find what we are looking for. When we have reduced the amount we own and store our documents all in the same place, we can tell at a glance whether we have it or not. If it's gone, we can shift gears immediately and start thinking about what to do. We can ask someone we know, call the company, or look up the information ourselves. Once we have come up with a solution, we have no choice but to act. And when we do, we notice that the problem is often solved surprisingly easily.

Instead of suffering from the stress of looking and not finding, we take action, and these actions often lead to unexpected benefits. When we search for the content elsewhere, we may discover new information. When we contact a friend, we may deepen that relationship or he or she may introduce us to someone who is well versed in the field. Repeated experiences like these teach us that if we take action we will be able to obtain the necessary information when we need it. **Life becomes far easier once you know that things will still work out even if you are lacking something.**

There is another reason that my clients never complain about discarding things—and this is the most significant. Because they have continued to identify and dispense with things that they don't need, they no longer abdicate responsibility for decision making to other people. When a problem arises, they don't look for some external cause or person to blame. They now make their own decisions and are aware that considering what action to take in any situation is what really matters. Selecting and discarding one's possessions is a continuous process of making decisions based on one's own values. Discarding hones one's decision-making skills. Isn't it a waste to squander the opportunity to develop this capacity by saving things? When I visit my clients' homes, I never throw anything away. I always leave the final decision up to them. If I chose what to discard for them, there would be no point in tidying. It is by putting one's own house in order that one's mind-set is changed.

Do you greet your house?

The first thing I do when I visit a client's home is to greet their house. I kneel formally on the floor in the center of the house and address the house in my mind. After giving a brief self-introduction, including my name, address, and occupation, I ask for help in creating a space where the family can enjoy a happier life. Then I bow. It is a silent ritual that only takes about two minutes, but it does elicit some strange looks from my clients.

I began this custom quite naturally based on the etiquette of worshipping at Shinto shrines. I don't remember exactly when I started doing it, but I believe I was inspired to do so because the tense expectancy in the air when a client opens the door resembles the atmosphere when one passes under a shrine gate and enters the sacred precincts. You may think that this ritual could only have a placebo effect, but I have noticed a real difference in the speed with which tidying occurs when I perform it.

Incidentally, I don't wear sweats or work clothes when I tidy. Instead, I usually wear a dress and blazer. Although occasionally I don an apron, my priority is on design over practicality. Some clients are surprised and worry that I might ruin my clothes, but I have no trouble moving furniture, climbing onto kitchen counters, and doing the other active work involved in tidying while dressed up. This is my way of showing respect for the house and its contents. **I believe that tidying is a celebration, a special send-off for those things that will be departing from the house, and therefore I dress accordingly.** I am confident that when I show respect by the clothes I choose to wear and begin the work of tidying by greeting the house, it will in turn be happy to tell me what the family no longer needs and where to put the things remaining so that the family can be comfortable and happy in this space. This attitude speeds up decision making at the storage stage and eliminates doubt from the entire tidying process so that everything flows more smoothly.

Perhaps you don't believe that you could do this. Perhaps you think you have to be a professional like me to hear what the house has to say. In fact, however, the owners understand their possessions and their house the best. As we progress through the lessons, my clients begin to see clearly what they need to discard and where things naturally belong, and the tidying work proceeds smoothly and speedily. There is one fail-proof strategy to quickly hone your sense of what you need and where things belong: greet your house every time you come home. This is the first homework assignment I give my clients at my private lessons. Just as you would greet your family or your pet, say, "Hello! I'm home," to your house when you return. If you forget when you walk in the door, then later, when you remember, say, "Thank you for giving me shelter." If you feel shy or embarrassed to say these things out loud, it is fine to say them silently in your mind.

If you do this repeatedly, you will start to feel your house respond when you come home. You will sense its pleasure passing through like a gentle breeze. Then you will gradually be able to feel where it would like you to tidy and where it would like you to put things. Carry on a dialogue with your home while tidying. I know this sounds totally impractical and fantastic, but if you ignore this step, you will find that the job goes less smoothly.

In essence, tidying ought to be the act of restoring balance among people, their possessions, and the house they live in. Conventional approaches to tidying, however, tend to focus solely on the relationship between people and their belongings and do not pay attention to their dwelling. I, however, am very conscious of the important role the house plays, because whenever I visit a client's home I can feel how much it cherishes its inhabitants. It is always there, waiting for my clients to return and standing ready to shelter and protect them. No matter how exhausted they are after a long day's work, it is there to refresh and heal them. When they don't feel like working and wander around the house in their birthday suit, the home accepts them just as they are. You won't find anyone more generous or welcoming than this. Tidying is our opportunity to express our appreciation to our home for all it does for us.

To test my theory, try putting your house in order from the perspective of what would make it happy. You will be surprised at how smoothly the decision-making process goes.

Your possessions want to help you

I have spent more than half my life thinking about tidying. I visit people's homes every day and spend time confronting their possessions. I do not think there is any other profession in which I would be able to see everything a person owns or examine the contents of closets and drawers, just as they are. Although I have visited many homes, naturally no one's possessions or way of organizing is identical. Yet all these possessions share one thing in common. Think about why you have the things you do. If you answer, "Because I chose them," "Because I need them," or "Because of a variety of coincidences," all of these responses would be correct. But without exception, all the things you own share the desire to be of use to you. I can say this with certainty because I have examined very carefully hundreds of thousands of possessions in my career as a tidying consultant.

When examined carefully, the fate that links us to the things we own is quite amazing. Take just one shirt, for example. Even if it was mass-produced in a factory, that particular shirt that you bought and brought home on that particular day is unique to you. The destiny that led us to each one of our possessions is just as precious and sacred as the destiny that connected us with the people in our lives. There is a reason why each one of your belongings came to you. When I share this perspective, some people say, "I neglected this outfit so long it's all wrinkled. It must be pretty indignant with me," or "If I don't use it, it will curse me." But from my own experience, I have never encountered any possession that reproached its owner. These thoughts stem from the owner's sense of guilt, not from the person's belongings. Then what do the things in our homes that don't spark joy actually feel? I think they simply want to leave. Lying forgotten in your closet, they know better than anyone else that they are not bringing joy to you now.

Everything you own wants to be of use to you. Even if you throw it away or burn it, it will only leave behind the energy of wanting to be of service. Freed from its physical form, it will move about your world as energy, letting other things know that you are a special person, and come back to you as the thing that will be of most use to who you are now, the thing that will bring you the most happiness.

A piece of clothing might come back as a new and beautiful outfit, or it may reappear as information or a new connection. I promise you: whatever you let go will come back in exactly the same amount, but only when it feels the desire to return to you. For this reason, when you part with something, don't sigh and say, "Oh, I never used this," or "Sorry I never got around to using you." Instead, send it off joyfully with words like, "Thank you for finding me," or "Have a good journey. See you again soon!"

Get rid of those things that no longer spark joy. **Make your parting a ceremony to launch them on a new journey.** Celebrate this occasion with them. I truly believe that our possessions are even happier and more vibrant when we let them go than when we first get them.

Your living space affects your body

Once the process of tidying is under way, many of my clients remark that they have lost weight or that they have firmed up their tummies. **It's a very strange phenomenon, but when we reduce what we own and essentially "detox" our house, it has a detox effect on our bodies as well.**

When we discard everything in one go, which sometimes means disposing of forty garbage bags of stuff in one day, our bodies may respond in a way that resembles a short fast. We may get a bout of diarrhea or break out in pimples. There is nothing wrong with this. Our bodies are just getting rid of toxins that have built up over the years, and they will be back to normal, or in fact in even better shape, within a day or two. One of my clients cleared out a closet and shed that she had neglected for ten years. Immediately after, she had a strong bout of diarrhea after which she felt much lighter. I know it sounds like false advertising to claim that you can lose weight by tidying or that it will make your skin clearer, but it is not necessarily untrue. Unfortunately, I can't show you before-and-after pictures of my clients, but I have witnessed with my own eyes how their appearance changes when their rooms are tidied. Their figures are more streamlined, their skin is more radiant, and their eyes shine brighter.

When I first started this business, I found this fact quite intriguing. But when I thought about it carefully, I realized that it isn't that strange. I think of it like this. When we put our house in order, the air inside becomes fresh and clean. Reducing the amount of stuff in our space also reduces the amount of dust, and we actually clean more often. When we can see the floor, the dirt stands out and we want to clean. Because clutter has been eliminated, it's much easier to clean and therefore we do it more thoroughly. The fresher air in the room must certainly be good for the skin. Cleaning involves energetic movement, which would naturally contribute to losing weight and staying fit. And when our space is completely clean, we don't have to worry about tidying, so we are free to focus on the next issue that is important in our lives.

Many people want to be slim and fit, and that becomes their focus. They start to walk longer distances and eat less junk food, and these actions contribute to weight loss without consciously dieting.

But I think the main reason tidying has this effect is because through this process people come to know contentment. After tidying, many clients tell me that their worldly desires have decreased. Whereas in the past, no matter how many clothes they had, they were never satisfied and always wanted something new to wear, once they selected and kept only those things that they really loved, they felt that they had everything they needed.

We amass material things for the same reason that we eat—to satisfy a craving. Buying on impulse and eating and drinking to excess are attempts to alleviate stress. From observing my clients, I have noticed that when they part with excess clothing, their tummies tend to slim down, when they discard books and documents, their minds tend to become clearer, when they reduce the number of cosmetics and tidy up the area around the sink and bath, their complexion tends to become clear and their skin smooth. Although I have no scientific basis for this theory, it is very interesting to see that the part of the body responding corresponds closely to the area that is put in order. Isn't it wonderful that tidying your house can also enhance your beauty and contribute to a healthier, trimmer body?

Is it true that tidying increases good fortune?

Due to the popularity of feng shui, people often ask me whether tidying will bring them good fortune. Feng shui is a method for increasing good fortune by organizing one's living environment. It began gaining in popularity in Japan about fifteen years ago and is now quite well known. For many people, feng shui is what first gets them interested in organizing and tidying their house. I am not a feng shui expert, but I did study the basics as part of my research on tidying. Whether or not you believe that it can improve your fortune is up to you, but since ancient times people in Japan have been applying their knowledge of feng shui and orientation principles to their daily lives.

I myself also apply the wisdom of our forebearers in my practice of tidying. For example, when I fold and stand clothes on edge in the drawer, I arrange them by color to form a gradation from dark to light. The proper order is to place clothes that are lighter in color at the front of the drawer and gradually progress to darker colors at the back. I don't know whether or not this increases good fortune, but when clothes are arranged in a gradation of color, it feels great to look at them whenever you open the drawer. For some reason, having lighter clothes at the front seems to have a calming effect. If you organize your living environment so that it feels comfortable and so that every day you feel energized and happy, wouldn't you say that your good fortune has increased?

The concepts underpinning feng shui are the dual forces of yin and yang and the five elements (metal, wood, water, fire, and earth). The basic belief is that everything has its own energy and that each thing should be treated in a way that suits its characteristics. To me, this seems perfectly natural. The philosophy of feng shui is really about living in accordance with the rules of nature. The purpose of my approach to tidying is exactly the same. The true purpose of tidying is, I believe, to live in the most natural state possible. Don't you think it is unnatural for us to possess things that don't bring us joy or things that we don't really need? I believe that owning only what we love and what we need is the most natural condition.

By putting our house in order, we can live in our natural state. We choose those things that bring us joy and cherish what is truly precious in our lives. Nothing can bring greater happiness than to be able to do something as simple and natural as this. If this is good fortune, then I am convinced that putting our house in order is the best way to achieve it.

How to identify what is truly precious

After a client has finished the process of selecting what to keep and what to discard, there are times when I will retrieve a few things from the "keep" pile and ask once again, "This T-shirt, and this sweater, here, do they really spark joy?"

With a look of surprise, my client inevitably says, "How did you know? Those are all things that I couldn't decide if I should keep or throw away."

I am not a fashion expert nor do I retrieve these things on the basis of how old they look. I can tell by my clients' expression when they are choosing—the way they hold the item, the gleam in their eyes when they touch it, the speed with which they decide. Their response is clearly different for things they like and things they are not sure of. When faced with something that brings joy, their decision is usually instantaneous, their touch is gentle, and their eyes shine. When faced with something that doesn't bring them joy, their hands pause, and they cock their head and frown. After thinking for a few moments, they throw the item onto the "keep" pile. At that moment, there is a tightness in their brow and around their lips. Joy manifests itself in the body, and I don't let these physical signs escape me.

To be honest, however, I can actually tell which items do not spark joy in my clients' hearts even without watching them during the selection process. Before I visit their homes, I give them a private lesson on the KonMari Method. This lecture alone has a significant impact, and often when I make my first visit to their house they have already begun tidying.

One of my prize students, a woman in her thirties, had discarded fifty garbage bags of belongings by the time I got there. She opened her drawers and closet proudly and said, "There's nothing more to get rid of in here!" Her room certainly looked different from the photographs she had shown me. The sweater that had been thrown carelessly over the dresser was now neatly stored away, and the dresses that had been jammed to bursting on the rod had been thinned out so that now there was some room between them. Yet even so, I pulled out a brown jacket and a beige blouse. They looked no different from the rest of the clothes she had decided to keep. Both were in good condition and looked like they had been worn.

"Do these really bring you joy?" I asked.

The expression on her face changed instantly. "That jacket, you know I love the design, but I really wanted one in black. They didn't have a black one in my size. . . . Not having a brown jacket, I thought that I would buy it anyway, but in the end it just didn't seem to suit me and I only wore it a few times.

"As for the blouse, I was really attracted to the design and to the material, so I actually bought two of them.

I wore the first one until it couldn't be worn, but for some reason I just don't seem to choose the second one anymore."

I had never seen how she treated these items nor did I know anything about the circumstances surrounding their purchase. All I did was observe carefully the clothes hanging in her closet. When you examine things closely, you can begin to discern whether or not those things bring their owner joy. When a woman is in love, the change in her is apparent to everyone around her. The love she receives from her partner, the confidence that love gives her, and her desire to make the effort to look beautiful for him all give her energy. Her skin glows, her eyes shine, and she becomes even more beautiful. In the same way, things that are loved by their owner and treated with care are vibrant and radiate an aura of wanting to be of more service to their owner. Things that are cherished shine. This is why I can tell at a glance whether something truly sparks joy. The genuine emotion of joy resides in the body and in the possessions of the owner, and therefore it can't be concealed.

Being surrounded by things that spark joy makes you happy

Everyone has things that they love, things that they cannot imagine parting with, even though other people shake their heads in disbelief when they see them. I see the things that other people find precious every day, and you would be amazed at the strange and incomprehensible articles that capture people's hearts—a set of ten finger puppets each with one eye only and every eye different, a broken alarm clock shaped like the Morinaga Noobow character, a driftwood collection that looks more like a heap of scrap wood. But the immediate response to my hesitant, "Does this . . . um, really spark joy?" is an emphatic "Yes!" There is no arguing with their confident gaze and shining eyes because I, too, have one such item: my Kiccoro T-shirt.

Kiccoro ("Forest Child") was one of two official mascots for Aichi Expo 2005, which promoted love for the earth and renewable, eco-friendly technology. The larger mascot, Morizo, is perhaps better known. Kiccoro was Morizo's sidekick, a little, lime green, roly-poly character, and my T-shirt shows only Kiccoro's face. I wear it around the house all the time. It is one thing that I just cannot bring myself to part with, even if people were to ridicule me, saying, "How can you keep this? Aren't you embarrassed? How can you wear that? You should throw it away."

Let me be clear. The clothes I wear at home are generally cute and pretty. I usually wear girly things, such as camisoles with layers of pink frills and flower-print cotton ensembles, around the house. The only exception is my Kiccoro T-shirt. It is quite a curious article, shocking green in color with just Kiccoro's eyes and half-open, full-lipped mouth, and the tag clearly indicates that it's a children's size. As the Expo was held in 2005, I've been wearing it for many years even though I have no sentimental memories from the event itself. Just reading what I've written here makes me feel embarrassed to be hanging on to such a thing, yet whenever I see it, I can't bring myself to throw it away. My heart starts beating faster as soon as I see Kiccoro's lovely round eyes.

The contents of my drawers are organized so that I can see at a glance what's there. This T-shirt sticks out like a sore thumb among all my graceful, feminine clothes, yet that just makes it more endearing. It's so old now, you would think that it would be stretched out of shape or stained, but it's not, so I can't find any excuse in that area for discarding it. The fact that the tag declares it was made in some other country even though it was a Japanese expo could have ruined its appeal for me, yet I still can't throw it away.

These are the types of things you should boldly hang on to. **If you can say without a doubt, "I really like this!" no matter what anyone else says, and if you like yourself for having it, then ignore what other people think.** To tell the truth, I would not want anyone else to see me wearing my Kiccoro T-shirt. But I keep it for the little joys it gives me, the giggle I get when I take it out and look at it all on my own, the contentment I feel when Kiccoro and I are sweating together as we clean and wondering what to tackle next.

I can think of no greater happiness in life than to be surrounded only by the things I love. How about you? All you need to do is to get rid of anything that doesn't touch your heart. There is no simpler way to contentment. What else could this be called but "the magic of tidying"?

Your real life begins after putting your house in order

Although I have spent this entire book talking about tidying, tidying is not actually necessary. You won't die if your house isn't tidy, and there are many people in the world who really don't care if they can't put their house in order. Such people, however, would never pick up this book. You, on the other hand, have been led by fate to read it, and that means you probably have a strong desire to change your current situation, to reset your life, to improve your lifestyle, to gain happiness, to shine. For this very reason, I can guarantee that you will be able to put your house in order. The moment you picked up this book with the intention of tidying, you took the first step. If you have read this far, you know what you need to do next.

Human beings can only truly cherish a limited number of things at one time. As I am both lazy and forgetful, I can't take proper care of too many things. That is why I want to cherish properly the things I love, and that is why I have insisted on tidying for so much of my life. I believe, however, that it is best to tidy up quickly and get it over with. Why? Because tidying is not the purpose of life.

If you think that tidying is something that must be done every day, if you think it is something that you will need to do all your life, it is time to wake up. I swear to you that tidying can be done thoroughly and quickly, all in one go. The only tasks that you will need to continue for the rest of your life are those of choosing what to keep and what to discard and of caring for the things you decide to keep. You can put your house in order now, once and forever. The only ones who need to spend their lives, year in and year out, thinking about tidying are people like me who find joy in it and who are passionate about using tidying to make the world a better place. **As for you, pour your time and passion into what brings you the most joy, your mission in life.** I am convinced that putting your house in order will help you find the mission that speaks to your heart. Life truly begins after you have put your house in order.

Afterword

The other day I woke up to find my neck and shoulders frozen stiff. I could not even get out of bed and had to call an ambulance. Although the cause was not clear, I had spent the previous day at a client's house, looking into the cupboard above the closet and moving heavy furniture. As I had not done anything else, the conclusion was that I had tidied too much. I must be the only patient to ever have "too much tidying" written on her medical record. Even so, as I lay in bed slowly regaining motion in my neck, 90 percent of my thoughts were about tidying. This experience made me appreciate the ability to look up into cupboards.

I wrote this book because I wanted to share the magic of tidying. The deep emotions in my heart when sending off things that have fulfilled their purpose, emotions much like those experienced at a graduation; the thrill I feel at the "click" of fate, when something finds where it is meant to be; and, best of all, the fresh, pure air that fills a room after it has been put in order—these are the things that make an ordinary day, with no special event, that much brighter.

I would like to take this opportunity to thank all those who supported me in writing this book when all I am really capable of is tidying—Mr. Takahashi of Sunmark Publishing, my family, all my possessions, my home. I pray that through the magic of tidying more people will be able to experience the joy and contentment of living surrounded by the things they love.

—Marie "KonMari" Kondo

About the author

Marie "KonMari" Kondo runs an acclaimed consulting business in Tokyo helping clients transform their cluttered homes into spaces of serenity and inspiration. With a three-month waiting list, her KonMari Method of decluttering and organizing has become an international phenomenon. *The Life-Changing Magic of Tidying Up* is a best seller in Japan, Germany, and the UK, with more than two million copies sold worldwide, and has been turned into a television drama for Japanese TV. She has been featured on more than thirty major Japanese television and radio programs and in the *London Times*, the *Sunday Times*, *Red* magazine, and *You* magazine, among others.

Index

Published in the United States by Ten Speed Press, an imprint of
the Crown Publishing Group, a division of Random House LLC,
a Penguin Random House Company, New York.
www.crownpublishing.com
www.tenspeed.com

Ten Speed Press and the Ten Speed Press colophon are registered trademarks
of Random House LLC.

Originally published in Japan as *Jinsei Ga Tokimeku Katazuke No Maho* by
Sunmark Publishing, Inc., Tokyo, in 2011. Copyright © 2011 by Marie Kondo.
English translation rights arranged with Sunmark Publishing, Inc., through
InterRights, Inc., Tokyo, Japan, and Waterside Productions Inc., California, USA.
This English translation by Cathy Hirano first published in Great Britain by
Ebury Publishing, an imprint of Random House UK, London.

Library of Congress Cataloging-in-Publication Data

Kondo, Marie, author.
  [Jinsei ga tokimeku katazuke no maho. English]
  The life-changing magic of tidying up : the Japanese art of decluttering
and organizing / Marie Kondo ; translated from Japanese by Cathy Hirano.
  — First North American edition.
      pages cm
  Includes index.
  1. Housekeeping. 2. Home economics. I. Title.
  TX321.K6613 2014
  648—dc23

                              2014017930

Hardcover ISBN: 978-1-60774-730-7
eBook ISBN: 978-1-60774-731-4

Printed in the United States of America

Design by Betsy Stromberg
Front cover image copyright © Vadim Georgiev/Shutterstock.com

50 49 48 47 46 45

First American Edition